the doctrine of GOD

Gary Farley

CONVENTION PRESS

About the Author

Gary Eugene Farley, professor and chairman of the Department of Sociology and Human Services at Carson-Newman College, Jefferson City, Tennessee, should not be a stranger to many of those who use Southern Baptist publications. For several years his writings have appeared frequently in curriculum materials and other SBC products. Now in his twelfth year at Carson-Newman College, Dr. Farley holds an M.A. in Sociology from the University of Tennessee, an M.Div. from Midwestern Baptist Theological Seminary, and a Th.D. in Social Ethics from Southwestern Baptist Theological Seminary.

Dr. Farley takes an active part in local politics in Jefferson City. At home he enjoys gardening and model trains. He and his wife Jackie have four children.

5133-14

This book is the text for a course
in the subject area Baptist Doctrine
in the Church Study Course

Dewey Decimal Classification Number: 231
Subject: GOD

Printed in the United States of America

Contents

Foreword

This is the first in a family of books that address themselves to some of the central doctrinal themes of the Christian faith and that are prepared especially for Southern Baptists. It is significant that in the Introduction to the first book of the family the author has included a brief definition of *doctrine*. The reader is led to consider the importance of studying doctrines, and an explanation is given of the way beliefs are shaped into a doctrine and doctrines into a theology.

In outlining his general objectives for those who study the book, Dr. Farley has stated five:

1. The learner should gain a well-rounded understanding of who God is. The purpose of the first five chapters is to communicate the multifaceted nature of God's person.

2. The learner should come to understand that God is a person and that the relationship of the believer to God and the mission of the church must be interpreted in the light of that fact.

3. The study should serve to introduce the learner to the heritage Baptists have in their various confessions of faith and statements of faith.

4. The entire study seeks to emphasize the beauty, truth, and deep spiritual insight of the Christian's daily worship.

5. As the process of interaction among learners takes place in the study of this book, the church should be built up.

BILL LATHAM

Three Ways to Study This Book

LARGE GROUP STUDY

This book is the text for Baptist Doctrine Week 1977. Most of the studies will be conducted in groups of twenty-five or more. These large group sessions will be more effective if the leader will use the suggestions in the *Baptist Doctrine Week Teaching and Promotion Kit* (Item 5143-14 on the Undated Materials Order Form).

SMALL GROUP STUDY

Church Training groups or other small groups can study this book by using the directions for leading small group sessions. These guides are at the end of the text and give directions for a one-hour session for each chapter. Each group determines the number of weeks in its study by selecting the chapters to be considered. If at all possible, all chapters should be studied in sequence.

INDIVIDUAL STUDY

You can study this book on your own as well as in a group. Carefully work through each chapter, completing each Personal Learning Activity as it appears in the text. You will be introduced to fresh ideas. Take time to consider and to evaluate each one.

Requirements for receiving credit in the Church Study Course for the study of this book are at the end of the text. *(See table of Contents.)*

Introduction

My father was a traveling salesman. I recall the good times we had planning his trips. With maps spread on the dining room table we would work out his week's itinerary of towns in which to call on his customers. We would talk about the experiences we had shared on other trips. Noting spots of possible difficulty and of unusual interest, we would select a route. Sometimes we considered alternate modes of transportation. I am sure that Dad mentally calculated whether the effort would be worth the cost.

The presentation of a book involves a similar procedure. The introduction to a book should be an invitation to come along on a journey. It offers a destination, indicates the mode of travel and route, and attempts to convince the prospective reader that the benefits coming to him will justify amply the costs involved. Also, in this introduction we shall consider some general facts about doctrines: why they are formed and why it is important to study them.

DESTINATION

The Doctrine of God is addressed to a specific audience. It is for you and other believers who are interested in rounding out your knowledge of and relationship with the God you worship. In your regular Bible study you probably have learned about one characteristic of God and then another. This may be your first opportunity to consider at one time all about who God is, what he does, and what he wills. Therefore, I have organized in a systematic and easily understood fashion some truths about God—truths learned by the faithful across the centuries through revelation, experience, and reflection.

Further, what you and I believe about God affects every aspect of our lives. Our understanding of what is happening in history; how we treat our families, friends, and enemies; how we go about doing our work; and even what we think about ourselves—all are grounded in what we believe about the nature, work, and will of God. Consequently, it is imperative for every Christian to try to know God as he really is.

MODE

The destination is a more complete understanding of God. How do I propose for us to travel there? There is no shortage of books about God. Check the shelves of a bookstore featuring religious literature or the holdings of a good library. Books about God come in at least six varieties, each type having a specific purpose and being addressed to a particular audience.

Some books about God are called apologies and are addressed to the curious, seekers for truth, and skeptical intellectuals. A second kind of book about God is historical and systematic theology. These studies are of great value for the professional theologian and the studious lay person. The third and fourth classes of books about God are devotional and practical in approach. A fifth category narrows its focus to some specific attribute, purpose, or activity of God. These books vary from the simple to the scholarly.

The final variety of books about God is the rarest. It is an exposition of what a Christian denomination affirms about God. *The Doctrine of God* is of this variety, the first such book for Southern Baptists. Of course, there is no Baptist God. You and I worship the same God as do other believers. However, Baptists have emphasized certain beliefs about God, such as God's freedom and personhood. This is where this book will place its stress.

To grasp what Baptists believe about God, we must study our statements of faith and confessions of faith, our hymns, the writings of our scholars, but most of all the Bible. I will assume that most readers of this book are already believers. I address the great masses of the faithful. I seek to edify, not to evangelize.

ROUTE

Baptists are a diverse, noncreedal people. How can anyone presume to speak for all Baptists? Fortunately, the nature of God has not been a point of controversy among us. Where differences appear, I will note the various positions; but the real focus is on the common elements. I will try to present our historic positions accurately. If there is anything new or unique in *The Doctrine of God*, it is the result of my special point of view, sociologist-theologian. Specifically, I plan to draw from the insights of "personality theory" to enrich the concept that God is person.

I have chosen lines from hymns and common prayer lines as the titles for most chapters. I believe that we affirm the great truths of our faith in and through the language of our everyday worship. I want to help you understand this language. As you study this book, it is not necessary for you to learn the strange tongue of scholarly theology. It will be enough for you to recognize the meanings of the lines you sing and pray.[1]

In addition, I will define the word *doctrine* and will present more fully the sources for information concerning what Baptists believe about God.

Believing, as I do, that our denomination owes its origin to the concept that God is free, chapter 1 is devoted to developing what "the freedom of God" means.

Chapters 2 through 4 deal with the other essential characteristics of God—great, good, and loving. Each chapter begins with an account of an experience from my life, probably similar to those of many of the readers. My purpose in this is to pull the concept being discussed down into the everyday world of believers. Each of these concepts is defined carefully and the related biblical teachings summarized. The chapters are tied together by the theme that the free God is person and must be known as such. This is the subject of chapter 5.

Chapter 6 deals with the statement of the doctrine of the Trinity found in the most recent Baptist statement of faith, "The Baptist Faith and Message."[2]

Chapter 7 deals with the everyday activities of God in relationship to people. Specifically, it deals with the question of how to understand God's providence in the light of evil and suffering in the world.

Chapter 8 focuses on the rock metaphor as a designation for God. It speaks of God's stability, strength, and salvation.

Ethics is the focus of chapter 9. What does God expect of us? How do we become like him?

In the conclusion I bring these elements together to present as full a picture of God as our limited understanding will allow.

COSTS—BENEFITS

The cost of coming on this journey can be limited to a few hours of reading the book, and five to ten sessions, discussing with friends its affirmations. However, if you are serious about the study, it may cost additional hours of reading, pondering, and seeking meanings for biblical passages. It may cost time spent in reading the classics of theology. It may even cost your present comprehension of God.

To lose your present understanding of the nature, work, and will of God can be costly unless it is replaced with a better and fuller understanding. Then the process can be considered an overall benefit.

The preparation of this text has been a growing experience for me. I have become painfully aware of the smallness of my concept of God and of my spiritual maturity. I now see him as a greater, better, more loving, more personal, more present God. Yet he remains, as he should, as the Baptists of London confessed in 1644:

> . . . God as he is in himselfe, cannot be comprehended of any but himselfe, dwelling in that inaccessible light, that no eye can attaine unto, whom never man saw, nor can see. . . .

My prayer is that you will have a similar experience.

This is where I am headed and how I plan to get there. I hope that I have convinced you to come along.[3] But before we begin our actual journey, I need to develop some boundaries for this project. Specifically, I need to define the terms of the title. What is doctrine? Who or what is God? Further, I will need to say more about the sources of information concerning what Baptists believe about God.

DOCTRINE: WHY STUDY IT?

What is *doctrine* and why should it be studied? "It sounds awfully stuffy to me," some will say. Often this is the case. It is hoped it will not be so here.

A *doctrine* is defined as "what is taught, particularly the principles of religion." A specific religion or denomination will hold beliefs about many topics, such as the nature of God, the meaning of human existence, salvation, worship, church organization, and eschatology or last things. When the beliefs about one of these topics are gathered together in a logical, coherent whole, this is called a doctrine. For example, Christians believe God to be free, holy, loving, creative, providential, and the like. When these beliefs are gathered together and analyzed in terms of one another, a doctrine of God is formulated. This is the same as building a house from many different stones, or perhaps making a cake by blending ingredients.

In turn, the various doctrines, that is, God, man, creation, redemption, church order, and last things, can be fashioned into a theology. A full discussion of a theology is normally an elaborate task that runs into several volumes. However, most denominations summarize their theology in an abbreviated statement of faith. Baptists call these statements of faith or confessions of faith.[4] The latest statement formulated and circulated widely among Southern Baptists is "The Baptist Faith and Message." Its purpose is to let people know what Southern Baptists, for the most part, believe, teach, and practice.

Beliefs are gathered together to form doctrine. Doctrines are collected to form a theology. From the theology a confession is drawn.

Baptists strive to keep doctrine from becoming a tradition that might stifle experience with the free working Spirit of God. Yet we realize that we can best test the spirits and more fully comprehend our religious experiences when they are framed by an understanding of doctrine.

RELIGION, DOCTRINE, AND GOD
I imagine that almost every author believes his subject to be the most important one in all the world. I certainly believe this to be true of the doctrine of God.

Definition of Religion
At the core of religion is a belief in a power or powers external to and greater than oneself, which can either help or harm. This power is comprehended in a variety of ways by different religions. Some declare that this power is personal—thinking,

willing, acting, feeling—and that the personal power has a name—God. Others worship an impersonal force—unbending and inscrutable. Some religions view this power as capricious. They worship a trickster whose greatest joy is doing harm to mankind. Others bow before a power that is known as dependable, trustworthy, faithful. In some instances the power is viewed as an all-powerful Lord. Others see the power as limited, suffering many of the same uncertainties that commonly affect mankind. Others depict the power as a genial genie anxious to do his worshipers a favor. In some religions the power is worshiped so that it might be placated; in others, so that it might be manipulated; in still others, so that its will might be comprehended and obeyed.

All of this is to say that the religious response of humankind to the power or powers, which lie outside themselves and which are greater than they, is most diffuse. If one studies world religions, he can find a great variety of things believed about God, or the gods. The systematic statement of these beliefs is for any given religion its doctrine of God.

The Christian Doctrine of God

The Christian doctrine of God is grounded in revelation—the self-revelation of God. Christians see the Bible as the record of God's revelation of himself to humankind. The Bible records the mighty acts of God in history. It records pronouncements by God about himself, his will, and his work. It records the responses of believers to this revelation in their worship. By studying this revelation believers have affirmed many beliefs about God, and these in turn have been collected and formulated into a doctrine of God.

DOCTRINE AND LIFE

What we believe makes a difference in how we act. A belief of great significance affects other beliefs. Doctrine should not be just theory. It should issue in practice. For example, what a person believes about the nature, work, and will of God affects all of his life.

First, the doctrine of God affects all other doctrines. What one believes about salvation, the end of time, church organization and polity, ethics, and the like is grounded in what he affirms about God.

Second, the everyday life of the Christian is shaped by his faith. The believer will set goals for his life and move toward them by means that are compatible with his doctrine of God. Likewise his world view and life-style are affected. His priorities, moral choices, and attitudes about life and death are based on this doctrine. The believer will interpret and respond to the crises of his life in terms of his understanding of who God is, what he wills, and how he acts.

Third, the task of Christian mission is facilitated by one's comprehension of God. Many who do not worship God have serious misconceptions about the nature, work, and will of God. Often the best place to begin in evangelism is to acknowledge that you, yourself, could not accept God as some nonbelievers see him. Then demonstrate how God is different from the way they see him. To use this approach to evangelism one must first have worked through what he believes about God.

Fourth, mature Christians have the responsibility of helping "babes in Christ" to grow and mature in their understanding of God by aiding them in interpreting God's will for their lives as well as in comprehending God's activity in the crises of life. This should be grounded in an accurate understanding of the doctrine of God.

Conversion, everyday living, maturity, and other doctrines are the reasons that understanding the doctrine of God is so important. This is why I believe that the doctrine of God is the most significant subject for Christians to study.

SOURCES

In researching what Baptists believe and teach about God one has four types of sources: formal statements, informal statements, empirical evidence, and the biblical revelation. From the very early days Baptists have been a confessing/confessional people. The study of Baptist confessions of faith is in itself an intriguing exercise. Usually those confessions were framed in response to some problem, such as persecution and misunderstanding from without or ignorance and heresy from within.

Formal Statements

John Smyth and Thomas Helwys prepared several confessions

at the turn of the seventeenth century. These were designed to make legitimate their doctrinal position to the authorities, civil and ecclesiastical. Since that time Baptists have formulated a number of confessions or statements of faith. Each time the purpose was to set forth clearly their doctrinal position at that time.

In addition to these widely accepted and used statements, some associations and churches have framed their own confessions of faith. A type of confession or statement of faith common to Baptist churches is a church covenant. Normally this is a very brief statement of faith and practice to which new members subscribe as they become members of the fellowship. Baptists also have had their systematic theologies written as expositions of the doctrines set forth in their statements of faith.

Informal Statements
In addition to these formal statements are the less formal affirmations about God found in hymns, prayer lines, autobiographies, and devotional literature. These provide a rich source of material for anyone interested in learning what Baptists believe about God.

Analysis of Beliefs
Another source is the empirical research (relying on experience or observation alone) of social scientists. In responding to questionnaires, what have Baptists confessed that they believe about God? Confessions and theologies state what one ought to believe. How do these stack up against the actual beliefs of Baptists?[5]

Biblical Revelation
Finally, the central and authoritative source of the doctrine of God for Baptists has been the Bible. Our statements of faith are laced liberally with references to biblical texts. God has made known his character, his work, and his will through pronouncements to his spokesmen and through his mighty acts in history. The acts and the self-affirmations confirm and clarify one another. Many Baptists agree with W. T. Conner that there was a developmental or progressive element in the Hebrews'

comprehension of the character and will of God. Thus Christ must be seen as the highest and most complete revelation of God.[6] And consequently all previous statements about God, as well as all subsequent ones, must be tested for accuracy by the revelation of God in Christ. In treating the biblical material as well as the formal and informal statements as will be done in each of the chapters to follow, care must be exercised to remain loyal to the revelation of God in Christ.

NOTES

1. Baptists are a singing people. Long ago when the preacher came to the community only once or twice a month, hymns were used as a means of instructing believers in the basic principles of the faith. Hymns continue to be an important source of the content of our belief. Hymn singing triggers remembrance of high religious moments. Hymns give utterance to the aspirations and concerns we may not verbalize in prayer. Hymns draw us back to the landmarks, the central affirmations of our faith.

Baptists are a praying people. Regular prayer services are an important part of the worship activities of Baptist churches. Some phrases have become rather standard in our public prayers. This standardization may be subjected to criticism, but at least it helps us give voice to our inward concerns.

2. Adopted at the annual meeting of the Southern Baptist Convention held in Kansas City, Missouri, 1963.

3. I want to express thanks to some of the people who are making this trip possible: T. B. Maston, Durery Patterson, Jim Bramlett, Morris Ashcraft, Walter Shurden, Herbert Miles, Jane Weeks, and others for reading and criticizing portions of this book; to my sociology of religion class for listening to parts of it; to Janie Huggins for checking syntax; to Jackie Farley for typing the manuscript; and to the Walter Turpins for providing a hideaway where I could commune with God.

4. William L. Lumpkin, *Baptist Confessions of Faith* (Philadelphia: The Judson Press, 1959), has rendered a great service by collecting many of the confessions of faith and interpreting them in terms of their historical setting.

5. Rodney Stark and Charles Y. Glock, *American Piety* (Berkley: University of California Press, 1968). This is only one of several that might be cited.

6. *Revelation and God*, pp. 103-45. Baptists would do well to reread this section in Conner's book.

Chapter 1

God Is Free

My students were excited about it, so I bought a copy of The
Lion, the Witch, and the Wardrobe, *Volume 1 of C. S.
Lewis' delightful Christian allegory* The Chronicles of
Narnia.[1] *With our six-year-old Clarissa in my lap before the
fire, I began to read it. I discovered that although she was
taken by the story, I was intrigued by the skill of this great
Christian apologist. In a most attractive and thought-
provoking way, he presented the central beliefs of the Christian
faith. It was while reading this book that I became impressed
with the centrality of the affirmation, God is free.
Thinking about this concept has done much to enhance
my appreciation of God.*

By way of introducing the basic concerns of this chapter, I am
sketching briefly the main features of *The Chronicles of Narnia*.
Lewis uses as his "type" for God, a great lion (Hos. 11:10),
Aslan. He is the great, mysterious creator of a universe that lies
in another dimension. Narnia, an island kingdom in that realm,
with all of its creatures has fallen into enslavement by the
forces of evil. The creatures long for the freedom promised to
them ages before, a freedom to be secured by Aslan's victory
over the forces of evil.

At long last Aslan brings four children from our world to
Narnia and works through them to call the creatures loyal to
him to join in battle with the evil ones. In the process Aslan
sacrificially allows himself to be taken captive, to suffer humiliation, and to die. Yet all is not lost. Aslan arises from the dead,
and he and the children and the good creatures of Narnia win
the victory. Lewis' recurrent theme is "Aslan is not a tame lion."

Through five more volumes Lewis develops this theme. The
creatures of Narnia suffer a variety of problems. Time after
time Aslan comes to aid his creatures. The reader is impressed

that Aslan is both to be feared and to be loved. This powerful, free being acts as he wills, when he wills, in the way he wills. Although he gives no merciful consideration to those who oppose him, he shows great affection in his care of those who obey him. Not infrequently his creatures grow impatient with him because they cannot understand his ways. They are painfully slow in learning that Aslan is not tame. Yet in time it becomes evident that his wisdom far exceeds theirs, and his way proves best.

In the seventh and final volume Aslan brings together his loyal friends from many of the earlier adventures. They enjoy a communal meal. Access to the tree of life is restored. Narnia is perfected. Victory is secured.

Our God, like Aslan in the story, is great, and good, and loving. As God moves history toward his goals, he demonstrates his freedom. God is not tame. He is sovereign. He is free. God is not like the genie of Aladdin's magic lamp and the gods of many pagan cultures. He does not respond to our beck and call, ready to do for us the service we require. He is not the "great vending machine" in the sky of some "popular" preachers, who declare that when one makes an offering to God, God is bound to respond by presenting the desired blessing. God is not our servant; rather we are to be his.

PERSONAL LEARNING ACTIVITY 1
Study John 3:1-3 and 8:25-32. Then write out how each expresses the greatness of God.

BAPTISTS AND THE FREEDOM OF GOD

Baptists should find the concept of the freedom of God attractive. Ask a Baptist in what way his beliefs differ from those of other Christians, and you likely will hear about separation of church and state, liberty of conscience, baptism of confessing persons by immersion, democratic church polity, or the autonomy of the local church. But, as Paul Harrison has contended ably, these doctrinal beliefs are derived from a more basic one—freedom of God.[2]

The Emergence of the Idea

Nearly four hundred years ago when John Smyth, Thomas

Helwys, John Murton, Roger Williams, John Clarke, and others were laying the foundation of the Baptist faith, their reasoning ran something like this: If God is Lord as all Christians confess, and if all people are personally responsible to God for their beliefs and actions, we must not allow barriers to be erected that frustrate the free working of his Spirit in the lives of persons. If people are forced to subscribe to a man-made creed, if people are forced to worship in a prescribed way, if people are allowed no freedom in making moral choices, God is not free to work as he wills. Consequently, the early Baptists argued that nothing should be allowed to stand in the way of God's freedom to call whom he wills to salvation, to the ministry of the gospel, to some special service. Further, the comprehension of God's Word must not be bound by tradition. God continues to speak to his people, providing new insights, rounding out old concepts, and offering guidance in new situations.

Specifically, these early Baptists demanded that civil rulers limit their authority to civil matters. They decried the formality of liturgical worship. They denounced creedalism. They were particularly harsh in their criticism of popes and bishops and ecclesiastical offices. Baptists were among the few who saw the old order of church and state intertwined as harmful to the free working of God's Spirit.

In short, Baptists saw the formal structures and traditional practices of religion in the established church to be an effort to tame God. They believed that the authorities wanted a god whom they could manipulate for national and personal interests. This, declared the early Baptists, is not the true understanding of the God of the Christian faith. Although the authorities were concerned that religion promote the solidarity of the society, the Baptists' primary concern was being faithful to the Scriptures. They found the central emphasis of the New Testament to fall on the salvation of persons. Consequently, they declared that the conversion of persons, not the maintenance of social solidarity, was the chief function of the church.

The Resultant Conflict
Of course, such freedom from traditional modes of authority runs the risk of degenerating into license, and of destroying the fragile fabric of social order. The Baptist leaders were re-

minded by the Established Church that such had been the case with some of their Anabaptist forerunners a century earlier in Europe. There extreme doctrines and practices had emerged. Cities and towns were thrown into chaos, yet those who instituted these practices argued that God's Spirit was the source of these new ways.

There were others who chided the Baptists for not going far enough. Quakers and more radical sects declared that all that Baptists were doing was replacing the tradition of the church with the tradition of the Bible. They asked, "Is not the Spirit of God still restricted?" These radicals had rejected all authority, except the "inner light" of the individual's spirit—a light from God, they claimed.

The Baptists' Response

Baptists responded to these challenges from the right and from the left by working out a new understanding of authority—one that does not allow tradition to keep God from being free, yet is protected from license (or abuse).

To the established church Baptists responded by asserting that the biblical revelation and specifically the life and teachings of Jesus provided the standard by which any claim of new insight must be measured. New doctrines and practices as well as the old should not depart from the plain teachings of the Scriptures.

To the radicals, Baptists countered that the revelation of God in Christ is fully adequate for salvation, for faith, and for practice. The Spirit is not to give new light, but to help in understanding and applying the old. As new situations emerge, ones for which the Scriptures offer no direct teachings, the Spirit of God will help believers know how the basic revelation can be applied appropriately. For example, the discovery that the world is not flat but more or less round, that we are but a small dot in a vast universe, that the process of creation is more complex than we once thought necessitated reinterpretation and modification of earlier doctrines. The Spirit assists in this assessment and reapplication. God remains the same; only our understanding and appreciation are subject to change. Baptists declared that because God is free, he communicates directly with the conscience of a person; and that person is responsible directly to God for what he believes and how he acts.

Baptists shared with the radicals a belief in the direct responsibility of the individual to God both for what he believed and for how he acted. They also shared an emphasis on God's direct communication to the conscience of the individual. Yet Baptists were wise enough and experienced enough to know that a person needs help both in discerning and in verifying God's revelation to his people. Help and support for the conscientious believer are offered by the congregation with which he is affiliated. For Baptists the local church is a second agency of God's free working. The fellowship provides a sounding board and feedback. It responds to one's interpretation of God's call to salvation, to ministry, to service. It votes on new members; it licenses and ordains ministers; it supports missions; it encourages people to use their spiritual gifts. The church also provides a setting where people can hammer out their understanding of theology and ethics. Often new insights come as a result of these discussions.

Realizing that whole congregations may, in the heat of conflict, misinterpret the teachings of God, Baptists created another level of assistance and support, the association. (The association is a group of churches in an area united to support common interests.) In an association church members and churches can seek the counsel of others on matters of faith and practice.[3]

Were Baptists guilty of taking away the freedom of God? No. Although a church might dismiss a member or an association might exclude a church with which there was a lack of agreement, this action did not mean that church or that person was "sent to hell." Although Baptists recognized the value of counsel from the church and from the association, they continued to maintain that a person's relationship to God is direct, person-to-person. Each believer is responsible for his faith and practice. Ministers, institutions, and traditions should not be allowed to interfere; rather they are to serve as facilitators. Perhaps the diagram at the end of this chapter best expresses this point.

By making the revelation of God in the Scriptures most important, Baptists were protected from license. By stressing that

God is free and speaks to individuals and to groups of individuals, they maintained the dynamic, living quality of the Scriptures. By restricting the authority of church tradition, they allowed God to be free. A free God must have free access to his creatures so that they too will be free and thus responsible for the way in which they respond to him.

Here is the heart of our faith. The free God must not be tamed by tradition. Yet God is dependable and provides us an accurate revelation of his person, work, and will in the Scriptures. Nothing can be allowed to stand in the way of God's freedom to work in the lives of persons. This is the reason that liberty of conscience is so precious to Baptists. We continue to be afraid of any tradition, old or new, that might thwart God's will. We want to be the free people of the free God.

Summary

To summarize, affirming the freedom of God is (1) to declare that he is not a deity subject to magical manipulation; (2) to demand that the movement of his Spirit must not be frustrated by interposing the church, tradition, or Scripture interpretations; and (3) to proclaim that God is a personal being, one who thinks, wills, and acts. Throughout *The Doctrine of God* a recurrent theme will be the freedom of God in all three of these dimensions. The freedom of God is a concept that helps in answering many of the problems some have with the Christian doctrine of God. It is a concept that must guide our formulation of theology and of practice. It is a concept that points us toward the true worship of God. God is free. The Baptist faith is grounded in this affirmation. But is this all that Baptists believe about God? No, our doctrine of God is comprised of other beliefs about him. We will study some of these beliefs in the following chapters.

PERSONAL LEARNING ACTIVITY 2
Now, explain in your own words how Baptists' belief in the freedom of God has affected their polity.

CONCLUSION

It is my hope that this chapter has made you aware of the centrality of the belief that God is free. For Baptists this is the fundamental assertion that led to the rejection of man-made and rigid authorities. Upon this belief are constructed Baptist distinctives such as liberty of conscience, believer's baptism, and democratic church organization.

Baptists reaffirmed the concept that God's Spirit deals directly with the spirits of persons. But realizing the active presence of evil in the world, Baptists determined that the Scriptures, particularly the life and work of Jesus, offer a test for claims of enlightenment by the Spirit. The church congregation is given an important role in equipping the believer, but it is not allowed to short-circuit the individual's responsibility to God. This was a significant reordering of the role of various authorities as they relate to the life of Christians.

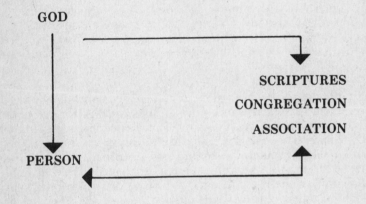

NOTES

1. The seven volumes of *The Chronicles of Narnia* are published by the Macmillan Company. They are available in paperback.

2. Paul Harrison, *Power and Authority in the Free Church Tradition* (Carbondale, Ill.: Southern Illinois University Press, 1959). Available in paperback, this is an important sociological study of the policy of American Baptists.

3. A. C. Underwood, *A History of the English Baptists* (London: The Carey Kingsgate Press Limited, 1947). Underwood presents a helpful discussion of the development of the Baptist faith in these early days.

Chapter 2

God Is Great

*At the family get-together Aunt Janie produced a dime from
her coin purse to reward curly-headed Gary Gene for reciting
the little prayer: "God is great. God is good. Let us thank him
for our food." I was pleased with the attention showered on me
by the grown-ups for my performance and with the balsam
wood glider I purchased with my dime.
Many years later as a grown-up myself and with children of
my own, I came to realize that the central affirmations of the
Christian faith are expressed in this simple prayer:
"God is great. God is good." These affirmations
provide the foundation of our faith.*

Our religion began with the pronouncement and demonstration of God's greatness in history as he entered into a covenant with Abraham. In the beginning God was concerned to show the Hebrews he was greater than the deities their neighbors worshiped. Through the events now recorded in the Bible the children of Israel came to realize that God is not only greater than these deities but that he *is* Deity, the only true God. All other gods were false. Today, in an age when many either deny the reality of God or live as though he has no power, believers must continue to affirm, "God is great."

MEANING OF GOD'S GREATNESS

What do we mean when we declare the greatness of God? Underlying our everyday usage is the feeling that something or some person is wonderful and powerful. The root meanings of the words of the Hebrew and Greek languages used to speak of the greatness of God indicate the same feeling: wealthy, gigantic in size, exciting, wonderful, powerful.

PERSONAL LEARNING ACTIVITY 3
Before studying further, write out your definition of
great. **Then study the Scriptures on the following**
page and write your explanation of what you think
Christians are saying when they declare that God is
great.

God is a great God. He is great because of what he does, because of who he is. He speaks of his greatness, and his acts confirm the truth of his statements.

In the introduction I made the point that religion is man's response to spiritual power that is greater than himself and that may either help or harm him. The Bible declares that God is this power.

Power can be defined as the capacities and resources one has at his disposal to accomplish his will, even in the face of opposition. This definition involves several important concepts that will undergird this study. First, this power is intentional. God wills. God has goals for his creation. God is employing his resources and capacities in the effort to achieve his goals.

Second, intentional power is personal power. God meets man person to person. In interpersonal relations one person gets the other to comply with his will though promise of reward, threat of punishment, or appeal to basic morality. God deals with humankind in all three of these modes. To the rebel, God's will comes with the threat of punishment and the promise of reward. To the saint, it comes with the appeal that doing God's will is exactly what ought to be done.

Third, God's power is Spirit power. Spirit—that is infinite— is not limited by time and space. Both rulers and nations die. Riches turn to dust. But God's power knows no limits other than limits that he might impose on himself.

Certainly our insistence on the freedom of God, our Baptist affirmation that God is not tame, is of importance here. A God who is not great is not of much use to people. The history of religion is strewn with the corpses of gods who proved to be powerless when their worshipers faced a crisis. Yet a god who is only powerful may be a tyrant. In this chapter I will focus on the greatness of God, but in following chapters this emphasis will be balanced by considering God's goodness and love.

PSALM 50

12 If I were hungry, I would not tell thee: for the world *is* mine, and the fulness thereof.

PSALM 66

5 Come and see the works of God: he *is* terrible *in his* doing toward the children of men.

PSALM 77

13 Thy way, O God, *is* in the sanctuary: who *is so* great a God as *our* God?

14 Thou *art* the God that doest wonders: thou hast declared thy strength among the people.

PSALM 135

5 For I know that the LORD *is* great, and *that* our Lord *is* above all gods.

6 Whatsoever the LORD pleased, *that* did he in heaven, and in earth, in the seas, and all deep places.

NUMBERS 23

23 Surely *there is* no enchantment against Jacob, neither *is there* any divination against Israel: according to this time it shall be said of Jacob and of Israel, What hath God wrought!

ISAIAH 40

22 *It is* he that sitteth upon the circle of the earth, and the inhabitants thereof *are* as grasshoppers; that stretcheth out the heavens as a curtain, and spreadeth them out as a tent to dwell in:

23 That bringeth the princes to nothing; he maketh the judges of the earth as vanity.

24 Yea, they shall not be planted; yea, they shall not be sown: yea, their stock shall not take root in the earth: and he shall also blow upon them, and they shall wither, and the whirlwind shall take them away as stubble.

25 To whom then will ye liken me, or shall I be equal? saith the Holy One.

26 Lift up your eyes on high, and behold who hath created these *things*, that bringeth out their host by number: he calleth them all by names by the greatness of his might, for that *he is* strong in power; not one faileth.

27 Why sayest thou, O Jacob, and speakest, O Israel, My way is hid from the LORD, and my judgment is passed over from my God?

28 ¶ Hast thou not known? hast thou not heard, *that* the everlasting God, the LORD, the Creator of the ends of the earth, fainteth not, neither is weary? *there is* no searching of his understanding.

29 He giveth power to the faint; and to *them that have* no might he increaseth strength.

30 Even the youths shall faint and be weary, and the young men shall utterly fall:

31 But they that wait upon the LORD shall renew *their* strength; they shall mount up with wings as eagles; they shall run, and not be weary; *and* they shall walk, and not faint.

GOD'S MIGHTY ACTS SHOW HIS GREATNESS

A variety of acts recorded in the Scriptures declare the greatness of God. These acts attest, or will attest, to the greatness of God, because to do these things requires the exercise of power, often in the face of opposition by other powers.

Creation

The Bible begins with the affirmation that God created the universe. This was not just reshaping matter that already existed, but rather calling matter into existence.[2] For the ancient Hebrew this must have been quite a feat. But for modern persons with our greater knowledge of the vastness and complexity of the universe, as well as the diversity of created beings and the balance and orderliness of nature, it defies comprehension.[3] Hebrew worship was characterized by expressions of joy and adoration to God for making such a wonderful universe (Pss. 104:1-31; 8:4; 33:5-9).

The greatness of Israel's God was demonstrated also by his maintenance of creation. Their God was not a master mechanic who got the universe running and then left it alone. The biblical God is one who is actively involved in the operation of creation (Col. 1:12-20; Heb. 1:1-4; 2 Pet. 1:3-4).

Throughout the Scriptures the greatness of God is cited as a motivation for people to submit themselves to him. Several such appeals are related to God's creative acts (Pss. 24:1-2; 100:1-3; Rev. 4:11 to 5:1).

His Acts in History

In biblical theology it has been popular to refer to the "mighty acts of God." Normally included among these are the Exodus, the Conquest, the Davidic kingship, and the Exile and Restoration. Common to these events is the fact that Hebrews were the unlikely victors in contests with great nations or the unlikely survivors of great catastrophe. History was the story of the powerful God accomplishing his purposes.[4]

Central among the mighty acts is that series of events occurring in the Exodus and Conquest. God chose a disorganized band of slaves and won their freedom from the greatest ruler on earth, Pharaoh of Egypt. This was no mean accomplishment. Working through his representative, Moses, God challenged the power of Pharaoh with a series of plagues.

And I will stretch out my hand, and smite Egypt with all my wonders which I will do in the midst thereof: and after that he will let you go (Ex. 3:20).

It has been stated that the ancient gods were the gods of the rich and powerful. Our Lord alone chose the weak, the poor, the outcasts. Whereas the other gods were the allies of the powerful in the exploitation of the weak, our God is first known as the champion and protector of the powerless. The lesson is plain. The powerful God has not chosen us because he needs us, but rather he has chosen us because he knows we need him.

Soon after mighty Pharaoh released the Hebrews, he changed his mind and with his army pursued them, desiring to enslave them again. In response to this treachery, God demonstrated his unrivaled power by causing the waters to part, enabling the Israelites to cross the sea safely. Then he allowed the waters to roll back, destroying the army of Egypt. The excitement and thankfulness of the Hebrews at the time of this event, as well as their awareness of the greatness of God, is caught by a song that they sang, glorifying God for giving them freedom (Ex. 15:1-19).

As the Hebrews passed into the wilderness, God continued to demonstrate his divine power and his presence by the cloud and the fire that guided and protected them (Ex. 13:21-22). At Sinai God used nature—thunder, lightning, and earthquake —to demonstrate his power (Ex. 19:16-20). As the biblical account continues by unfolding the story of the Hebrews' unfaithfulness, lack of trust, and misunderstanding of God's will, one sees that they still had much to learn about God. In spite of their unfaithfulness, the great God kept on blessing this slave people whom he had redeemed. He made a new covenant with them. He obligated himself to give them the land that he had promised to their ancestor Abraham (Ex. 34:8-14). As they began their assault on the Canaanites, God is depicted as fighting alongside his people, giving them success (Ex. 14:25; 15:3; Deut. 3:22; Josh. 10:13-14; Judg. 4:23; 5:11). Balaam, the Moabite magician, comprehended the greatness of God when he declared:

> God is not man. . . . God brought them out of Egypt; he hath as it were the strength of an unicorn. Surely there is no enchantment against Jacob, neither is there any divination against Israel: according to this time it shall be said of Jacob and of Israel, What hath God wrought! (Num. 23:19-23).

Once in the Promised Land, the Hebrew people continued to be blessed by God. When other peoples sought to take the land from them and place them in servitude, God raised up a series of leaders who rallied the people and won victories over the oppressors (Judg. 5). Still later God provided the nation with the leadership of David and his son Solomon. These kings unified the nation and made it a power in the world of its day. The worship of the Hebrews, as reflected in their songs from this era, proclaimed the greatness of God (Pss. 86:8; 89:6-11; 135:5-6).

Yet the life of the Hebrews in Palestine was not characterized by unmixed success. The nation split into two kingdoms after Solomon. Powerful neighboring countries extended their influence over Israel and Judah. War was not uncommon. The people were not true to God; they were attracted by nature deities and their sensuous worship. They attempted to mix the worship of God with the worship of foreign cults. Some Hebrews became rich by exploiting the poor. Consequently, the nation began to learn of another side of God's greatness —redemptive punishment (Isa. 25:1-2).

The prophets urged the Hebrew people to trust in the Lord and worship him only (Isa. 3:8; 10:15-18; Lam. 3:40-42). He alone was great. He could save his people as he had done in the past they declared. In some instances, as during the reign of Josiah, the people did respond to this message (2 Kings 22—23). Finally, God caused Israel and Judah to be defeated, and many of their people were carried into captivity by Assyria and Babylon. It would have been easy to interpret these events as defeats of God, and consequently to believe that he was not as powerful as the gods of these nations. Instead, the prophets instructed the people to learn some new lessons from this bitter experience.

First, their God is not a national God, limited to a particular territory. Their great God is Lord of all. He can use the power of those who do not even know him to accomplish his purposes. Second, God will bring a remnant of the nation back to the Promised Land and reestablish his people. This further attests his greatness. Third, by doing this God will impress on the people that he has chosen Israel for a missionary purpose—to call all people to the worship of the true God. This is the message of Isaiah, Jeremiah, Ezekiel, and Jonah.

Incarnation

Truly the incarnation was an event that demonstrated God's great power. God's powerful Word by which he created the universe became flesh (John 1:1-14). For this accomplishment this great force chose to divest itself of its power by accepting the limitations of time and space, finitude (Phil. 2:5-11). Only a personage of great power could choose to lay aside his power.

The virgin birth was a demonstration of marvelous power, as were the accompanying signs and wonders. Power also manifested itself in many ways in the life of Jesus. The power of God was demonstrated by the miracles he performed. Jesus' life was one of continuing conflict between himself and the demonic forces (Luke 4:1-13). His message was the coming of God's kingdom in power and judgment (Matt. 25). He was a model of obedience, always obedient to God's will, depending on God for power and guidance (Luke 22:42).

The death of Jesus was accompanied by demonstrations of God's power over nature (Matt. 27:45-54). One interpretation of the cross is to see in it the victory of Christ over sin, death, and the law (Rom. 7). Briefly, this interpretation is that throughout his life the demonic forces had attempted to get Jesus to sin by rejecting the will of God as revealed in the law. Their ultimate weapon was the threat of death. But having killed Jesus, they lost any possibility they might have had to defeat him. Thus God by divesting himself of his power and coming in the flesh and subjecting himself to temptation set the stage for the great victory. His invitation to us is to share in his victory by believing that he had indeed won even in the face of the continuing presence of sin and death and the working of demonic forces on earth.[5]

The resurrection and ascension of Jesus were also events of great power. They were the demonstrations to the believers that God in Christ had indeed won the victory. They marked a shift in the role of God's Son. He is pictured as resuming his place of power (Phil. 2:9-11), as serving as our High Priest (Heb. 7—9), and as preparing to come with his kingdom in power (Matt. 25).

The Kingdom

Jesus proclaimed the kingdom. By employing this concept he declared the sovereignty of God over all creation, over all history, over all humankind. But Jesus gave this concept a special meaning. First, God is Lord in a unique way over those who acknowledge his claims to be sovereign now. In light of the world situation, to respond calls for an act of faith. We give evidence that God is our Lord as we keep his commandments (John 15—17).

The church as described in the New Testament recognized this unique sovereignty of God. And God furnished the believers with spiritual power and special gifts so that the church might be built up, so that evidence might be provided to unbelievers that the Lord of the church is truly a powerful God (the Acts and the epistles of Paul).

The church also anticipated the time when Christ would come in power to establish the kingdom on earth, the second special meaning of the kingdom. This event was pictured as a time when the forces of evil would be totally defeated, creation perfected, evil punished, and the righteous rewarded (Matt. 25; 1 Cor. 15; Rev.).[6]

PERSONAL LEARNING ACTIVITY 4
Review the four mighty acts that have been discussed. In the margin beside each write how you feel that act expressed God's powerfulness as well as his greatness.

GOD'S ROLES SHOW HIS GREATNESS
People know other people through the roles they perform. And this is a way we learn about God. When the student of the Bible reads seeking to learn about God, he cannot help being impressed by the repeated testimony to the greatness of God's acts. Yet as God acts in history, he performs many roles —Creator, Sustainer, King, Judge, Perfecter, and Father. Each of these roles serves as a showcase of God's character, and in turn manifests his unequaled power.

In the section on the acts of God I noted that God is Creator, Sustainer, and Perfecter of the universe. Theologians have devoted much attention to how much one can learn about God from nature. Certainly creation attests to the greatness of God. For some it provides a foundation for monotheism—the Creator God must be sovereign.

King

For Israel, the role of God which spoke most eloquently of his greatness was that he is King. Kings were great personages. Their courts were characterized by displays of great wealth. Precious metals, jewels, and rich drapings decorated their halls. Bountiful meals graced their tables. The scent of rich perfumes hung in the air. Their words became law. They exerted great authority over the life and property of their subjects. The hearts of common folk overflowed with awe when they were in their presence. Many psalms picture God as a rich and powerful king (Pss. 99—104).

God's claim to the role of King is grounded in the fact that he founded the nation by redeeming the Hebrews from slavery (2 Sam. 7:22-23). This act was made necessary by a still earlier act, God's covenant with Abraham (Gen. 12:1-3; Ex. 6:2-4). Scholars have noted that there are two kinds of covenants in the old world: one is between equals, and the other between the great person and those who are subordinate to him. God's covenant with Abraham is of the second type. This means that the great God freely chose to enter into this relationship. The covenant was renewed at Sinai, and the people chose to agree to the demands of the covenant (Ex. 19:8). Moses stressed the importance of this relationship by reminding the Hebrews that God had freely chosen them (Deut. 9:5-8).[7]

The New Testament also emphasizes that God is King, although the focus is on Christ's coming in glory (Matt. 25:34; 1 Tim. 1:17). Paul declared that at the end of time Christ will come again, be victorious over Satan, and then the Father will reign supreme (1 Cor. 15:24-28). The New Testament also speaks of a covenant relationship between God and his people (Heb. 8:6-13; 12:24). Like the earlier one it is between God and those he has chosen to be subordinate to him. Also like the earlier one the subjects are invited to acknowledge his dominance.

In recent years there have been those who have wanted to democratize God because they found a sovereign God distasteful. Certainly God is more than King; he is not pictured as King alone. But the concept speaks correctly of God's power, majesty, rule, sovereignty, and freedom. It must be an integral part of any doctrine of God. Further, in the face of the evil and suffering that characterize our age, it offers a necessary hope: the King is coming![8]

Judge

A closely related role of God is that of Judge (Ps. 98:9). Judgment is a kingly privilege (1 Kings 3:16-28). The authority of judges rested in their appointment by the king. Judges had great power over the life and property of persons brought before their court. In the New Testament Jesus is pictured as a Judge at the end of time. (Matt. 25:32). This role will be given greater attention in the next chapter.

Father

Another role of God that shows God's power is Father (Lev. 19:2; Hos. 11:1-3). Old Testament law spelled out rights and duties for the father (Num. 30:3-5; Deut. 21:15-21). The father in the Old Testament could exercise great power over his household. He was the first line of social order. The father was to be the dominant person, and other family members were to be subordinate to him. In using the image of father to speak about the character of God, something of the power of the father was intended (Deut. 8:5-6). Father became the primary designation of God in the Gospels (Matt. 5—7).

Before concluding this section note must be made that many of the roles of power introduced in the Old Testament to speak of God are reapplied to Jesus in the New Testament (Father is the exception). This practice testifies to the belief of the church that Jesus was God come in the flesh. Also it testifies to belief in the preexistence of Christ. The reason for the exception is that Jesus declared his subordination to God the Father (John 12:27-28,49-50; 17:1-5). And as Son he is identified with both the plight of man and the hope of man to become heir with Christ (Rom. 8:17). Christ is the mediator, the bridge between the Father and his sinful creatures (1 Tim. 2:5).

PERSONAL LEARNING ACTIVITY 5

Of the three roles attributed to God, which do you feel best expresses his greatness? Write the reason in the margin beside that role.

GOD'S PERSONALITY TRAITS SHOW HIS GREATNESS

It is widely held that a person's conduct is grounded in his personality. "By their fruits ye shall know them" (Matt. 7:20). Conduct and character cannot be separated.[9] Having noted greatness in the acts of God and in the roles he performs, one can conclude that he is a great person. What are the personal characteristics of God that denote his greatness? Certainly included must be holiness, glory, righteousness, wisdom, mystery, and power. These are not his only qualities, nor do they speak exclusively of greatness. Not everyone counted great in our society can boast these qualities; but these must be the basis of any definition of true greatness of person.

Holy

Imagine that day Isaiah met God in the Temple at Jerusalem.

> In the year that king Uzziah died I saw the Lord sitting upon a throne, high and lifted up, and his train filled the temple. Above it stood the seraphims . . . . And one cried unto another and said, Holy, holy, holy, is the Lord of hosts: the whole earth is full of his glory. And the posts of the door moved at the voice of him that cried, and the house was filled with smoke. Then said I, Woe is me! for I am undone; because I am a man of unclean lips, and I dwell in the midst of a people of unclean lips: for mine eyes have seen the King, the Lord of hosts (Isa. 6:1-5).

This experience speaks volumes about the holiness of God. God appears as a king, one more powerful, more majestic than any earthly king before or since. Brightness, the shaking of the earth, and clouds of smoke accompany his self-revelation. The seraphim guard the person of God and bar unauthorized access, protecting his purity. They announce his holiness. The contrast is so great that Isaiah, perhaps for the first time, becomes aware of his smallness, weakness, and impurity. He realizes that when compared with God, this is the condition of all people.

The biblical concept of holiness emphasizes uniqueness. God is unique in two senses. First, he is uncontaminated, unapproachable, "wholly other" in his person. Second, he is morally pure in his relations with others. Only the pure, ritually and ethically, can stand before God (Ps. 24). In the case of Isaiah God cleansed and commissioned (Isa. 6:4-8). This is true in our case as well. All our righteousness is as filthy rags (Isa. 64:6). God must act upon us if we are to be pure (Isa. 8:6).

Old Testament scholar Theodorus Vriezen contends that the idea of God's holiness is the central concept of Hebrew religion. God is a great God. The ancient rabbis did not dare to pronounce his name. They feared for their lives when performing sacred ritual. Reverent awe, not chumminess, characterized their relationship with God.[10] Rudolph Otto adds that a dread of god is a universal characteristic of religion.[11] Yet humankind seems to be drawn to that which it dreads. The ironic social phenomenon of the summer of 1975 was people waiting for hours in long lines and collectively paying out millions of dollars to be scared out of their wits by the movie *Jaws*. Frightened as they might have been by the display of great power on the screen, they were drawn like moths to the light. Likewise the awesome holiness of God attracts.

The unlimited power, or holiness, of God is the message of the book of Job. Chapters 38—41 present a series of contrasts between the puny power of Job and the awesome power of God. Perhaps the key statement of God's holiness appears in Hosea.

> For I am God and not man, the Holy One in your midst (Hos. 11:9, RSV).

Although the holy God is pure, separate, and moral, he is still the God who comes in love to save his people. Hosea continues, catching something of the attractiveness of awesome holiness.

> They shall go after the Lord, he will roar like a lion; yea, he will roar, and his sons shall come trembling from the west; they shall come trembling like birds from Egypt . . . (Hos. 11:10-11, RSV).

Glory
In Isaiah's vision of God in the Temple (Isa. 6), the glory of God testified to his holiness. Glory seems to have three, perhaps four, meanings in the Scriptures. One is brightness or

radiance as in Isaiah's vision. This also would seem to be the
meaning of God's glory in the account of Moses' looking upon
him (Ex. 33:19-23). Elsewhere glory refers to wealth (Gen.
45:13; 1 Chron. 22:5). Christ's revelation of God includes both
these usages (Heb. 1:3; 2:6; John 1:14; 17:4; Jas. 2:1). Paul
picked up the idea that Jesus sought to glorify the Father (John
1:14; 7:15-19; 17:4; Heb. 1:3) and declared that we also are to
glorify the Father through Christ (2 Cor. 1:20-22). By so doing
his brightness is reflected, his richness confirmed. Perhaps
building upon Psalm 24 glory becomes a proper noun, meaning the same as heaven. The transfiguration of Jesus (Matt.
17:2) should be interpreted as a manifestation of his divinity by
revealing his radiant glory (Rom. 6:4; 1 Pet. 1:21; 2 Tim. 3:16;
Acts 2:33; Phil. 2:9-11). Other passages proclaim that Christ
will come again in power and glory (Matt. 24:30 to 25:31; 1
Thess. 4:16-17).

As a characteristic of God's personality, glory denotes majestic power, attractiveness, uniqueness, and richness. Again our
God is so wonderful that we stand in awe of him, yet we feel
compelled to draw near to him, to bask in his glory, to live lives
that honor him and inspire others to glorify him.

Righteous
One aspect of the holiness of God is his righteousness, and that
righteousness is also a quality of his greatness. God can be good
because he is so great. Often we are petty, we seek revenge,
and we are not straightforward because we are unsure of ourselves. God knows that he is the greatest. There is no reason
for him to be mean. I may be tempted to get even with someone because I feel threatened by him. God cannot be
threatened by any of us puny folk. When God speaks of being
jealous (Ex. 20:5), it does not mean that he inordinately fears
that we may take away his power. Rather, his jealousy shows his
sense of rightness. Man's proper function is to serve God.
When we fail to do so, God is hurt, disappointed, and sorrow-
ful.

The dependability of God speaks of the positive side of God's
righteousness. God can be steady and dependable, because he
can handle whatever comes. He cannot be scared, tempted, or
forced into some rash action. He is the Lord.

Wise

The great God, who is not limited by time and space, is pictured as wise (Isa. 55:6-9). He sees what remains hidden to us. He not only sees but comprehends completely. Then he acts. And his acts are designed to achieve his ultimate purposes.

God looks behind the masks we wear. And although we may fool others and even ourselves concerning our intents, he knows, he judges, he responds (Luke 16:14-15).

Paul contended that true wisdom comes from God (1 Cor. 1:20-26). He stated that the Spirit of God knows the secrets of God and is revealing them to the believers (1 Cor. 2:7-13). God gives spiritual insight to believers so they can understand the truth he has for them (Eph. 1:17-23). John also made much of the truth. Jesus comes as the Word "full of grace and truth" (John 1:14). We must worship the Father in "spirit and in truth" (John 4:23-24). Jesus bears witness to the truth (John 5:33). The truth will free us (John 8:32). Jesus is the truth (John 14:6). The Spirit is the truth (1 John 5:6). The great men on the human scene have been those with access to knowledge not available to everyone. Certainly the fact that God is wise, that he is truth, declares his greatness. That he shares his truth and wisdom with us is indicative of his love.

Powerful

Throughout this study I have identified God's greatness with his power. David's blessing summarizes much of the biblical witness to the power of God.

> "Blessed art thou, O Lord, the God of Israel our father, for ever and ever. Thine, O Lord, is the greatness, and the power, and the glory, and the victory, and the majesty; for all that is in the heavens and in the earth is thine; thine is the kingdom, O Lord, and thou art exalted as head above all" (1 Chron. 29:10-11, RSV).

This statement makes use of the roles of King and Father. It is grounded in God's mighty acts in history. It speaks of the qualities of glory, power, and greatness. It declares what man's response to God must be.

God has not only the resources of power but also the capacity to use it. Many rulers have had the resources of power but have lacked the wisdom or the resolve to exercise it effectively. God's mighty acts in history speak of a person who does not shrink before the problems of using power. God has a will for history, and he acts positively to bring it to pass.

Still another point must be made. Jesus gave new meaning to power. Traditionally, men have thought of the powerful as those who dominate. But Jesus came as Servant (Isa. 53). He requires the same of his followers (John 13:13-18). He demonstrated that the staying power of love is greater than that of the sword.

Mysterious

Many great Christians have testified that the more they have come to know God, the more they realized they could not understand him completely. This is as it should be. Some persons lack depth. In a brief encounter you learn all there is about them that is worth knowing. Their attractiveness is lost. With others, each encounter is a new adventure. New horizons, new vistas of their personhood present themselves. Of God the psalmist said:

> God is the Lord, and greatly to be praised, and his greatness is unsearchable. One generation shall laud thy works to another, and shall declare thy mighty acts (Ps. 145:3-4, RSV).

Paul added:

> O the depth of the riches and wisdom and knowledge of God! How unsearchable are his judgments and how inscrutable his way! "For who has known the mind of the Lord, or who has been his counselor?" (Rom. 11:33-34, RSV).

Such is the richness of God's person. And this makes him all the more attractive.[12]

PERSONAL LEARNING ACTIVITY 6
Write a short paragraph explaining what impact you feel the belief that God is great should have in the everyday lives of those who worship him.

CONCLUSION

Words, specifically words in my mind, have proved to be inadequate to express the greatness of God. But in this chapter we have had the benefit of the testimony of Isaiah, Paul, and others to the greatness of God. An experience common to many has been the thrill of singing with a great crusade throng, "How Great Thou Art." We listen to the other thousands; we join in and blend our testimony with theirs; memories of God's great acts flood our minds; God's powerful presence is real to our spirits; we sense that we are being confirmed in our faith; we know that our lack of comprehension and our doubts are not all that important. God is a great God.

In this chapter I have shown that God was known by Israel and by the early church as the great God. This was because of what he had to say about himself, what he did, and the roles he performed. Building upon this revelation believers have come to comprehend his character. Certainly personality traits were grounded in his greatness. Perhaps the designation *Lord* best characterizes God's greatness.

Rather than fretting about the philosophical questions of evil, suffering, predestination, and the like, let us learn the lesson of the letter to the Hebrews. Beset by problems, the Hebrews were threatening to turn back to Old Testament worship. So the writer of Hebrews stresses again and again that the great God is sufficient. Let us acknowledge our subordination to God. If we as Christians can learn this lesson, we shall be able to cope with life as it comes.

NOTES

1. Most of the scriptural quotations in this book are from the Revised Standard Version. In a few instances familiar passages are quoted from the King James Version.

2. The reference here is the traditional Christian doctrine of creation *ex nihilo*. See Augustus Hopkins Strong, *Systematic Theology* (Philadelphia: The Judson Press, 1907), pp. 371-410.

3. Among the attempts by Christian apologists to deal with this topic are Pierre Teilhard de Chardin's *The Phenomenon of Man* (New York: Harper & Row, Publishers, Inc., 1959); Karl Heim's *Christian Faith and Natural Science* (New York: Harper & Row, Publishers, Inc., 1957); and Langdon Gilkey's *Maker of Heaven and Earth* (Garden City: Doubleday & Co., Inc., 1959).

4. Serious students are referred to George Ernest Wright and R. H. Fuller's *The Book of the Acts of God* (Garden City: Doubleday & Co.,

Inc., 1957); William Foxwell Albright's *From the Stone Age to Christianity* (Baltimore: The John Hopkins Press, 1940); or John Bright's *A History of Israel* (Philadelphia: The Westminster Press, 1959).

5. Serious students are referred to Gustaf Aulén, *Christus Victor* (New York: The Macmillan Co., 1961).

6. See George Eldon Ladd, *The Gospel of the Kingdom: Scripture Studies in the Kingdom of God* (Grand Rapids: William B. Eerdmans Publishing Co., 1959); and Dale Moody, *The Hope of Glory* (Grand Rapids: William B. Eerdmans Publishing Co., 1964).

7. See "Covenant," *Zondervan Pictorial Encyclopedia of the Bible*.

8. See Walter Thomas Conner, *Revelation and God* (Nashville: Broadman Press, 1936), p. 244.

9. This concept will be developed more fully in chapter 5.

10. Theodorus Christiaan Vriezen, *Outline of Old Testament Theology*, tr. from the Dutch by S. Neuijen (Veenman, 1958).

11. Rudolf Otto, *The Idea of the Holy*, tr. by John W. Harvey (New York: Oxford University Press, 1958).

12. Most books on the doctrine of God devote much of their attention to such things as the attributes of God, the decrees of God, proofs of God's existence, and critical problems with the belief in God. Early in its history when the church began to gain a foothold in the Greco-Roman world, it adopted the language of current philosophy and translated the gospel into philosophical terms. The purpose was to make Christianity intellectually respectable. Once beliefs were formulated into philosophical categories, questions of logic had to be framed. Examples of these questions are: How can God be everywhere at a given moment? What was before God? Why did an all-powerful God allow sin to come into his world? Does God not grow through his experiences with humankind? Attempts to answer such questions as these caused lengthy debates within the church.

The problem is that concentration on such questions turned Christian theology from the central issue. The church forgot that God is person and persons are not things that should be subjected to logical analysis. People are to be encountered and experienced. To demand that God's behavior meet the standards of logic is to change him into a computer. No, thank you.

Please do not accuse me of attempting to hide God and make it more difficult to understand him. My point is that much theology had obscured the person of God. The purpose of theology should be the knowledge of God as a person, not the obscuring of God by a lot of philosophical speculation.

Chapter 3

God Is Good

The Egyptians believed Ra was a great god. As a sun-god he
blessed the nation with its great bounty. He appeared as the
head of the family of gods. The Babylonians believed Marduk
was a great god. They thought he created the world. He was
pictured presenting the law to Hammurabi. Marduk gave the
armies of Babylon victory. Zeus or Jupiter was the great sky
god of the Greeks and Romans. He too was great in war and
in maintenance of social order. Jehovah (or Yahweh) was the
god of the Hebrews. Also a great god, he differed from the
others by not being willing to share his authority and
power with other deities.

An important difference distinguished Jehovah from the
pagan gods. Although other gods might yield to humanlike
frailties and seduce a woman, accept a bribe, or treat their
subjects unpredictably, only Jehovah was good. No wonder the
Hebrews were a "stiff-necked and stubborn people, doubting
God." Never before had humankind known a God who was
both great and good.[1]

MEANING OF GOD'S GOODNESS

In everyday language *good* serves a variety of purposes. Think
of some of the ways you use *good*. Here is my list. *Good* is used
frequently to indicate that something is pleasing to the senses.
This looks, tastes, feels, smells, sounds—good. Sometimes *good*
is employed to indicate something that does not quite measure
up to our standard for greatness. For example, it was a good
game—not a great one. *Good* may be used also to suggest flexibility in a person. This is what is meant when someone is referred to as a "good old boy"; that is, he can be counted on to
go along with the crowd. Certainly the best usage in everyday

PSALMS 119

65 Thou hast dealt well with thy servant,
O LORD, according to thy word.
66 Teach me good judgment and knowledge,
for I believe in thy commandments.

PSALMS 25

8 Good and upright is the LORD;
therefore he instructs sinners in the way.
9 He leads the humble in what is right,
and teaches the humble his way.
10 All the paths of the LORD are steadfast love and faithfulness,
for those who keep his covenant and his testimonies.

PSALMS 143

10 Teach me to do thy will,
for thou art my God!
Let thy good spirit lead me
on a level path!

PSALM 100

5 For the LORD is good;
his steadfast love endures for ever,
and his faithfulness to all generations.

DEUTERONOMY 32

4 "The Rock, his work is perfect;
for all his ways are justice.
A God of faithfulness and without iniquity,
just and right is he.

ROMANS 11

22 Note then the kindness and the severity of God: severity toward those who have fallen, but God's kindness to you, provided you continue in his kindness; otherwise you too will be cut off.

MICAH

8 He has showed you, O man, what is good;
and what does the LORD require of you
but to do justice, and to love kindness,
and to walk humbly with your God?

LUKE 11

13 If you then, who are evil, know how to give good gifts to your children, how much more will the heavenly Father give the Holy Spirit to those who ask him!"

PSALMS 9

7 But the LORD sits enthroned for ever,
he has established his throne for judgment;
8 and he judges the world with righteousness,
he judges the peoples with equity.

JOHN 10

14 I am the good shepherd; I know my own and my own know me, 15 as the Father knows me and I know the Father; and I lay down my life for the sheep.

AMOS 5

24 But let justice roll down like waters,
and righteousness like an ever-flowing stream.

RSV

life is to refer to the moral qualities of integrity and righteousness. When one uses—*good* in this way, he means that a person is dependable, trustworthy, faithful, and morally circumspect. And then, *good* can be used also to mean kind. An example of this usage might be when one says to a visitor, "It was good of you to come." This listing of meanings is only a sampling of the many meanings attached to the word. It is apparent that defining *good* is not easy.

So, what are we saying when we pray, "God is good"? My guess is that the typical worshiper has the kindness of God in mind. The believer is saying, "Thank you, God, for providing food, shelter, friends, joy, meaning for life, and salvation." The focus is on the many acts of kindness of God. These reveal his goodness. Perhaps a few even intend the prayer line as a slap on the back for their "cosmic chum." However, the purpose of this chapter is to demonstrate that the most basic meaning of the statement "God is good" is as a reference to the holiness and righteousness of his person and the justice of his acts.

Jesus said, " 'No one is good but God alone' " (Mark 10:18, RSV). Just as it was the claim of moral goodness that distinguished Jehovah from the false deities of other nations, so it is his perfect goodness that separates him from us.[2]

PERSONAL LEARNING ACTIVITY 7
Study the Scriptures on the opposite page. Underscore words and phrases that show God's holiness, righteousness, moral purity, and justice.

Many other passages speak of God's goodness. The clear teaching of the Scriptures is that God is good. Several important ideas can be drawn from this central point. First, God is the one who defines what the good is. Second, the Christian affirms, although he does not understand fully, that God's governing of history is good because it is consistent with his personality. Third, we affirm that in his dealings with his people, God reveals himself to be dependable, trustworthy, and just. His acts are the standard of integrity. Fourth, God's laws and commandments define the good. Read the psalmist's definition of the good man:

Blessed is the man who walks not in the counsel of the
wicked, nor stands in the ways of sinners, nor sits in the seat
of scoffers; but his delight is in the law of the Lord, and on
his law he meditates day and night (Ps. 1:1-2, RSV).

Fifth, the good God is known in the social role of righteous
Judge. As Judge, God pronounces judgment upon humankind
in terms of punishment and reward.

Of course, the belief that God is good frequently is challenged by those who are concerned with the presence of evil
and suffering in the world. However, if it is true that God is the
one who defines what is good and what is evil, it follows that we
are not to begin with our own definition of the good or goodness and then judge God. This is the classical error of both
philosophical ethics and popular morality. God is God. We are
his creatures. He defines good. We comprehend the good by
comprehending him.

This is a lesson most people yet have to learn. Probably,
everyone of us has heard people ask questions such as these: If
God is good, why has he allowed this suffering to come into my
life? If God is good, why did he allow Hitler to order the
murder of six million Jews? If God is good, why did he cause
the Managua earthquake? If God is good, why . . . ? A believer
can respond by speaking of the nature of God's plan for redemption of man and the universe, of freedom and responsibility, or of the power of the demonic forces. But these answers
are seldom fully satisfactory.

The central point is this: In asking questions of this type, the
questioners are beginning with their own definition of good
and then judging God. Is it not the message of Genesis 3 that
humankind sinned initially by wanting to define for himself
good and evil? Humankind continues to want to be like the
gods.

Of course, honest doubt and questioning play an important
part in spiritual growth. By wondering how the good God
could cause or allow certain things to happen, one may gain
greater insight into the nature and work of God. This was the
case with Job and Habbakkuk. But when I define the good,
which is God's exclusive right, and judge him deficient, I sin.

This chapter counteracts any tendency to see God as a good

old boy or a doting grandfather. By studying God's mighty acts, his roles, his commandments, and his pronouncements about himself, we will learn of his righteousness and love. Humankind must take seriously the fact that God is good.

GOD'S MIGHTY ACTS SHOW HIS GOODNESS

The acts that depict God's greatness, as presented in chapter 2, also show God's moral goodness. So we will look at many of the same events, but our focus will shift.

In considering the goodness of God's acts, I will focus on his global acts—creation, fall and punishment, the old covenant, law and punishment, incarnation and the new covenant, and coming judgment.

Creation

The statement "And God saw that it was good" (Gen. 1:10,12,18,21,25) runs through the creation story. After creating man and considering the whole of creation, God's assessment seemed to be heightened, and he declared, "It was very good" (Gen. 1:31). Perhaps God was referring only to the beauty of his handiwork. Perhaps he was concerned that the Hebrews he warned not to accept the dualism of the Persians and some Greeks who saw matter as evil and spirit as good. Perhaps he meant goodness in the sense of orderliness and dependability in contrast with the pagan picture of an unpredictable creation full of spirits who are notoriously fickle. Perhaps he meant that as the good God he had created a universe and peopled it with morally responsible persons who would be responsive to his will, exercising authority over nature as his stewards (Gen. 1:29-30; 2:15). Perhaps all of these lie behind God's declaration of the goodness of his work.

The Fall and Punishment

In the garden was the tree of the knowledge of good and evil. God forbade that man eat of that tree. Apparently, the lesson was that mankind must recognize his place as subservient to God by depending on him for the definition of good and evil, as well as for life itself.

The fall, of course, was not the act of God. Man rebelliously sought to define good and evil for himself. God responded by driving him from the garden, making his life less pleasant, and blocking his access to the tree of life.

But mankind did not take heed. Cain slew Abel; Lamech slew another. The writer comments, "Now the earth was corrupt in God's sight, and the earth was filled with violence" (Gen. 6:11, RSV). God was disturbed by mankind's disobedience (Gen. 6:6). But the tower of Babel and a flood that destroyed civilization (Gen. 7 to 11:9) seem to have changed mankind little in his rebellion against the sovereignty of God. Mankind continued to want to define the good for himself.

The Old Covenant
The good God did not give up on man. He called on Abram and offered him a covenant (Gen. 12:1-3). He promised him property, prestige, and protection. Abram responded by accepting God's offer, leaving his kin, and moving with his household into a strange, alien land. Some years passed; Abram had been successful, but he had no son for an heir. So God covenanted with him to give him a son. The covenant was formally ratified in the customary manner (Gen. 15:1-11). Later, a third covenant was made (Gen. 17:1-16) in which Abram became Abraham. The sign of the covenant was circumcision of male children. And an ethical imperative was added: " 'Walk before me, and be blameless' " (Gen. 17:1, RSV). Finally a son was born to Abraham and Sarah when they were old. God had begun to fulfill the promises of the covenant.

But why did God make Abraham wait so long for an heir? Why did God choose and stick with a character as flawed morally as Abraham? Why did God use circumcision as the sign of the covenant? It was necessary for Abraham to learn that God is great and good. His sins against Pharaoh and Abimelech with Sarah (Gen. 12; 20) and against Hagar and Ishmael (Gen. 16; 21) were sins of impatience and lack of dependence on God. The high spot in the development of Abraham came when he had learned enough about God that he would risk sacrificing his only heir (Gen. 22). On this occasion God renewed the covenant (Gen. 22:15-18). Abraham's act demonstrated his faith in the power of God to give him another heir, and his willingness to let God define the good. Circumcision was a wonderful symbol of the covenant because it demonstrated man's confidence in God to be great and good enough to keep his covenant to make a great nation.[3]

Paul, interpreting the covenant, picked up on the statement, "And he believed the Lord; and he reckoned it to him as righteousness" (Gen. 15:6, RSV; Rom. 4). This is why God made a covenant—to teach men that God is dependable. And having learned this, men are to respond by keeping the way of the Lord and " 'by doing righteousness and justice" ' (Gen. 18:19, RSV). Abraham's faith was not in a creed or in a belief in the existence of God, but rather it was faith in God's integrity and his ability to do what he had promised.

Throughout the Old Testament God is pictured as keeping his part of the covenant. He called Israel out of Egypt because he remembered his covenant (Ex. 2:23-25). He made possible the conquest of the Promised Land (Josh.). He made the nation a world power. He brought a remnant back from the Babylonian captivity. And in Jesus he blessed the world beyond measure. So let us underscore in our minds that a basic element in the idea that God is good is his *dependability* reflected in the old covenant.

Law and Punishment

The good, dependable God was no trickster. It was enough for him to have Abraham teach his children principles of righteousness and justice. In a family setting what is just and right is readily evident. But when Israel became a nation characterized by interfamily, intertribal, and international relations, there was a need for amplification and application of the principles of justice and righteousness. God wanted the people to know what he expected of them. So at Sinai God gave his covenant people the law. The giving of the law was framed by a renewing of the covenant between God and his people (Ex. 19).

The core of that law was the Ten Commandments (Ex. 20:1-17). Included in those Commandments were regulations for the proper attitude toward and worship of God. Also included were laws that provide a basis for social order in any society. The sanctity of family, property, reputation, truth, and life were declared. God prohibited coveting, knowing that the source of evil acts is the desire of the mind.

Other passages containing the law of ancient Israel are to be

seen as the application of these basic principles to the moral
conduct of the nation in everyday life (Ex. 21—23; Deut.
12—26). Of particular interest for this study of the doctrine of
God is the holiness code found in Leviticus 17—26. Here the
clear emphasis is on treating all people justly (Lev. 19:15-18).
Perhaps the ethical high watermark of the Old Testament is
the statement found in this code. " 'You shall be holy; for I the
Lord your God am holy' " (Lev. 19:1, RSV).

The severity of the punishment for the crimes mentioned in
this code, in many cases calling for death, indicates something
of the seriousness of the idea that God's people are to be holy
people. Further, there is more to being holy than keeping law.
The Lord is the model. And he is good in his essence.

Now let us underscore three other ideas: (1) God defines
what is good by providing the law. (2) Giving of the law is a
good act—we can know what God expects of us. (3) God is our
model for goodness.

But the people did break the covenant (Ezek. 39:24-25).
Even with the help of the law the people failed to do God's will.

PERSONAL LEARNING ACTIVITY 8
In these Scripture passages find and list the
specific charges the prophets made against Israel:
Exodus 32:9-10; Joshua 24:16-20; Amos 3:1-2;
Malachi 3:7-9; Psalm 11:4-7; Amos 4; 5:11,13;
Malachi 2:14; Micah 6:7-8; Isaiah 1:11.

What choice did the good God have but to punish the nation
for its badness? Recall how concerned you have been for youth
making mistakes that will affect their lives adversely. Perhaps
you have used a variety of tactics—promised reward, advice,
encouragement, threats, and punishment—in an effort to get
them back on the right track. Could God do less?

Let us take note of two more ideas: (1) God takes our conduct seriously. (2) The biblical God used punishment as a
means to a redemptive purpose; not as a vindictive response of
his injured pride.

In the national history of the Hebrews as recorded in the Old
Testament one finds a pattern of God's blessing, the people
straying, God's warning of punishment, evil continuing, calam-

ity coming in the form of defeat or dominations by a foreign power, and after a while God's restoring the nation and giving it another chance (Ps. 78). Punishment also might be personalized. Many of the psalms either request God to punish the evildoers (Pss. 5; 10; 12; 37) or to forgive the sins of the worshiper (Pss. 51; 79).

Of course, we Americans view punishment as un-American. Suffering is to be shunned. Can it have redemptive value? I think that my favorite Indian medicine man, Black Elk, was closer to the truth when he said: "You have noticed that the truth comes into this world with two faces. One is sad with suffering, and the other laughs; but it is the same face, laughing or weeping."[4] He explains that when we are happy, it may take a sad experience to get through to us, and vice versa. It is the contrast that arrests us. Sometimes the only way God can teach us truth is to shake us so badly that we see the inadequacy of our understanding and are made ready for new truth.

This concept underscores the importance of believers studying the doctrine of God. We may be spared some hard knocks, because we have learned what God wants us to know. When events out of the ordinary come, we can interpret them more correctly only if we have an adequate understanding of the nature, work, and will of God.

Incarnation and New Covenant

Normally, the incarnation is thought of as being a demonstration of God's love. But it also can be considered a demonstration of God's greatness, as was shown in chapter 2, and as evidence of God's goodness (Heb. 6—11).

In Hebrews 8 the writer quoted God's promise (Jer. 31: 31-34) that he would make a new covenant with his people. The new was to differ from the old in that the law, God's moral expectations, would be internalized, written on the heart. People have always had problems with laws. Humankind has perverted the intent of laws given as guidelines for goodness. Humankind has been ingenious in devising ways of shunning the law. Consequently, laws become an opportunity for greater perverseness, rather than accomplishing their intended purpose of promoting goodness. God in the new covenant quickens in believers a sense of oughtness, a conscience that will help them to do the good. This will be a more effective control than a law code, because violation triggers feelings of guilt.

The new covenant differs from the old in that God's Spirit is an ever present, indwelling reality. Under the old, God's Spirit came only upon certain chosen persons for special purposes. God seemed to be far away. In the new every believer is to have fellowship with God. His Spirit and ours communicate. He directs, empowers, teaches, and comforts.

The new was to differ from the old in that the believer would have the assurance of cleansing. Formerly, one might come to the Temple and offer a sacrifice but never know whether he had been forgiven. But with the new the sense of forgiveness, of cleansing, of joy in salvation becomes a reality.

How is this new covenant effected? Jesus as the High Priest offers himself as a sacrifice. The holiness and righteousness of God is demonstrated by the costliness of the new covenant to him. In the resurrection Jesus instituted the new covenant (Heb. 7—10).

How does one become a party to the new covenant? As with the old, by faith (Heb. 11). One must believe that Jesus is sufficient; that he is powerful enough to do what he has promised to do; that he is dependable.

Paul made much the same point in his letter to the Romans (Rom. 2—4). Christ made manifest the righteousness of God. He ratified the new covenant by his blood. It became effective for us through faith. The Lord's Supper, like baptism, became a sign of the new covenant (Matt. 26:27-28).

Final Judgment

In writing to the Christians in Thessalonica Paul assured them that their suffering would be rewarded. When God established his kingdom, things would be made right (2 Thess. 1:55). Jesus (Matt. 25) pictured an eschatological judgment at which time the good will be rewarded for their deeds and the bad punished.

The essential point is that God being just and righteous takes our actions seriously. Those who remain in rebellion must be punished. The good must be rewarded. What else might a righteous and just God do? Would the alternative of no punishment and/or universal salvation be just?

Many people of good will have questions about what God will do under certain unusual circumstances. Questions such as these are best left to God. He is the Judge, not we. Our responsibility is to warn and to help prepare people for the judgment.

PERSONAL LEARNING ACTIVITY 9
You have studied six of God's acts that show his goodness. In the presentation of each, the author gave at least one important point or idea that he said should be emphasized. How many can you recall? Find and underscore these points or ideas.

GOD'S ROLES SHOW HIS GOODNESS
God is the righteous King and the just Father. He is a teacher of goodness (Isa. 30:19-21). But the role most frequently used to describe God's goodness is Judge. This is especially true in the Old Testament.

The integrity of the judicial system is what holds a nation together. The courts must offer hope for relief from wrongs. The prophets were harsh in their criticism of corrupt judges (Amos 5:15). The image of the ideal judge is that of a person who is concerned that justice be done. He follows the law. He is impartial. He considers all the facts and reaches the best verdict possible. (Yet in fixing punishment he will be merciful and take into account unusual circumstances.)

The book of Isaiah opens with a court scene. God is the Judge. Charges are brought against the nation. Then God admonishes them:

> "Wash yourselves; make yourselves clean; remove the evil of your doings from before my eyes; cease to do evil, learn to do good; seek justice, correct oppression; defend the fatherless, plead for the widow.

> "Come now, let us reason together, says the Lord: though your sins are like scarlet, they shall be as white as snow; though they are red like crimson, they shall become like wool" (Isa. 1:16-18, RSV).

Jeremiah and the psalmist also picture God as the just and righteous, holy Judge (Jer. 17:9-10; 31:29-30; Pss. 58:11;

75:6-8; 76:8). It is evident that God expects his people to be good people. We are to treat others justly. The good Judge offers to cleanse us. He offers insight into what it means to be just and righteous.

Jesus declared that at the end of time he will come as King and judge the nations (Matt. 25:31-46). His standard of judgment will be righteousness (Acts 17:31).

GOD'S CHARACTERISTICS SHOW HIS GOODNESS

God is good. I have demonstrated that the acts of God display the quality of goodness. I have considered how the major social roles, particularly Judge, that are used to characterize God's dealings with mankind, are good. Now note that many of his personality characteristics show his goodness.

Holy

In chapter 2 it was noted that *holy* means the purity of God in both the sense of separateness and distinction from mankind and in the sense of moral correctness. One of the ways Jehovah was different from the pagan gods was his moral qualities. The moral purity of God is demonstrated by these facts: (1) He defines what is good. (2) He does what he defines as good. Neither of these points should be neglected. On several occasions holiness and perfection are attributed to God (Lev. 19:2; Matt. 5:48; Heb. 12:14).

Righteous and Just

Righteous is the way God is in himself; just is the way he is known in his dealings with his creatures. By using these terms together one is declaring something more. Some distinguish between the motivation or intention of an act and the result of an act. In his relationship with humankind the righteous God acts justly. Good motive and consequences are brought together. If a person is righteous in his character, his treatment of others is just. This is the point of several teachings by Jesus that declare that the quality of a plant and the fruit it produces are vitally related (Mark 11:12-18; 11:27 to 12:12; John 15:1-14).

Many biblical passages speak of the righteousness and justice of God (Ps. 71:19; Isa. 5:16; Jer. 23:6; Pss. 101:1; 103:6;

45:6-7). Others declare that believers should take on these qualities (1 John 2:29; Rom. 3:5-7) and act accordingly (Amos 5:21).

Certainly the idea that God is not partial is evident in the discussions of God's justice (Deut. 10:17-18; Jer. 5:4-5; Rom. 2:11; Ps. 37:30-34). Fairness and uprightness are other concepts that seem apparent. I find that distinguishing among God's roles as King, Father, and Judge helps me understand his righteousness and justice. As King he is the legislator who formulates basic moral principles. He defines what is right and good. As Father he interacts with people. In these encounters believers come to recognize justice and righteousness as qualities of his person. We recognize these qualities both in the consistency of his acts with the rules he has formulated and in the feeling we have about the way God has dealt with us (fairly and impartially). As Judge God condemns us and with all fairness judges us guilty of transgressing the laws of God. Yet if we respond, he stands ready to forgive us. In redemption we are justified. He helps us understand what is expected of us, and he helps us become righteous (Rom. 2—6).

Dependable

God is called faithful (Ps. 36; 1 Cor. 1:9; 1 John 1:9) and truthful (Ps. 43:3; Isa. 28:29). Frequently he is referred to as a rock (Pss. 18:2,46; 19:14; 31:2; 62:2). The rock concept is that God is dependable; he can be counted on to be and to do what he says. Another term that is descriptive of the same quality is integrity. (See chap. 8.)

So often we find that great men have faults. But not God. Even our faithfulness cannot cause God to be or to do other than he is (Rom. 8:34). God is strong. God keeps his promises. He lets us know what he expects of us. He tells it like it is. We know where he is.

Good people are drawn to the person who has integrity. We may be attracted by the con man for a time. But the relationship soon will become offensive. Further, when one enters into a relationship with the dependable God, he can expect the relationship to grow.

PERSONAL LEARNING ACTIVITY 10
Recall and consider the characteristics that you studied. Then list them in what you consider their order of importance in showing the goodness of God.

ETHICAL IMPLICATIONS

Christianity had been called the great ethical religion. Its high moral demands are grounded in the belief that God is good. The core of Christian ethics is the demand that believers cultivate in their lives the same moral qualities that characterize the person of God whom they worship (Lev. 19:2; Matt. 5:48; 1 Tim. 5:21; 1 John 2:29; 3:2).

The essential purpose of our relation is to restore a proper relationship between God and man. In turn, our relationship with others and with ourselves is improved. The covenant that defines this relationship calls on us to do two things. First, we are to exercise faith that God is both powerful enough and dependable enough to do for us what he has promised. Second, we are to keep his commandments (1 John). We may do this in part because of fear and in part because of gratitude. We are to look forward to the time when God appears, because then we will be perfected. In the meantime, we strive toward being like our model, God, as revealed in Christ (1 John 3:2-3).

Realizing the vital relation between the tree and its fruits, we attempt to develop, with God's help, qualities of righteousness, truthfulness, integrity, and love. We continue to analyze our acts in terms of the standards of justice and righteousness. We learn from our sins. God helps us to mature and to be more like him.

To take seriously the command of Jesus that we be perfect even as our heavenly Father (Matt. 5:48), means that we will never be fully satisfied with ourselves.

CONCLUSION

A major concern of this chapter was to stress the moral goodness of God. This was distinguished from his kindness. God acts with integrity. He is dependable.

Some have a problem with the idea that God is good. So I

have stressed the concept that God is good in himself. And as God it is he, not we, who defines the good. When everything is finished, we will see that all God has done was good. And the evil that he allowed has been corrected.

The role of God that best illustrates his goodness—especially in the Old Testament—is that of Judge. It is important to stress this function. Some say that modern man does not recognize this role of God. Perhaps. But it is to our sorrow if we do not.

It is important to look at both the Abrahamic and the new covenants in this chapter. God gives a covenant because he is good. He establishes an orderly relationship with us. He keeps his part of the covenant. He holds us accountable for ours.

Coupled with this is the ethical emphasis that we are to be good like God. We are to be persons of integrity, dependability, truthfulness, and essential goodness. The gracious God helps us to grow toward the maturity he demands of us.

NOTES

1. George Ernest Wright and R. H. Fuller, *The Book of the Acts of God* (Garden City: Doubleday & Co., Inc., 1957), stress this point.

2. Walter Thomas Conner, *Revelation and God* (Nashville: Broadman Press, 1936), provides a helpful discussion of the holiness and righteousness of God. Augustus Hopkins Strong, *Systematic Theology* (Philadelphia: The Judson Press, 1907), discusses the holiness of God.

3. "Circumcision," Merrill C. Tenney, ed., *The Zondervan Pictorial Encyclopedia of the Bible*.

Chapter 4

"Praise Him . . . God Is Love"

*It was a dark and dank basement, but Mrs. Sherman Button's
Sunday School Primary Department met there, and I liked to
attend. For opening exercises she regularly presented a Bible
quiz. By the second or third year most of us had learned the
answers by heart. And we would sing so loudly that sometimes
someone would come to quieten us. It was there in the company
of my friends that I learned to sing about the love of
God–words such as, "Jesus loves the little children . . ." or
"Praise him, Praise him, all ye little children, God is love,
God is love."
Mrs. Button and her co-workers drilled us on our memory
verses: "Love one another"; "Love thy neighbour as thyself";
"God is love"; "Thou shalt love the Lord thy God . . ."; "For
God so loved the world . . ."; and others. I still remember how
these affirmations seemed so important to our teachers and
how proud I was of myself for learning to repeat them.*

Perhaps I am reading back into those experiences too much,
but it seems to me that I learned these truths from Mrs. Button: (1) I should not be selfish (and this was hard to live by in
the secular world of the Francis Willard Elementary School
playground across the street from the church). (2) The greatest
personage anywhere, God, loved me enough to sacrifice his
Son so that I would not have to go to hell. (3) I should love God
for loving me as I loved my parents and my kin (and I did love
my kin, because family was important to me).

Certainly God will have some special rewards for all the Mrs.
Buttons who showed the love of God to children like me. Of
course, the antics of my cohorts, Bill and Herbert Pritchard,
Ogle Lester Cunningham, Freddy Merrill, Bobby Brown,
Stewart Hock, and James Bybee made whatever stars that are
placed in our teachers' crowns well-deserved.

They tried to teach us about God. In retelling the biblical stories of David, Jonathan, Moses, Samuel, Paul, and others, I am sure that they spoke of God's being a mighty Lord and a righteous Judge, but the image of God that fixed itself in my mind was that of a loving Father. And it was this image of God that took control of my mind and heart at Easter. I could do no other thing than to commit my life to him. And I think I felt a little different the next time when Freddy, Herbie, Stewart, Bobby, and I, and all the others sang, "Praise him . . . God is love."

MEANING OF GOD'S LOVE

Like the words *great* and *good*, perhaps even more so, the word *love* has many meanings. Frequently, we use *love* to refer to those things and persons that give us pleasure. I love (like) Mexican food, football, and politics; and I love all those people who treat me the way I want to be treated. One of the reasons I love my family and my God is that they give me pleasure. This kind of love is not innately bad. In fact, it may be good. It seems that God created things so that they would afford pleasure. A taste for food, beauty, success, security, or learning is God-given, and we should appreciate and enjoy these tastes.

However, those things and related activities that give us pleasure often provide an occasion for temptation and for sin. To love (like) and take pleasure in those things that are not pleasing to God is wrong. To make some pleasure(s) one's ultimate concern (god) is wrong. To use other people as means (things) by which to achieve pleasure is wrong.

Consider sex. God gave people sex drives and made sex relations pleasurable so that the race might survive and couples might be bonded together by memory and expectation of pleasurable relationships. But when persons seek to enjoy sex in wrong ways, the sex drive becomes the occasion for sin. The Greeks called this type of love *eros*. Our popular culture has made much of this kind of love in songs, literature, and drama. Frequently, the church in condemning the misuse of sensuous pleasure has made the error of condemning pleasure per se.

A second meaning of love is from the Greek word *phileo* and refers to the sense of bonding, of community, of common in-

7 Beloved, let us love one another; for love is of God, and he who loves is born of God and knows God. [8] He who does not love does not know God; for God is love. [9] In this the love of God was made manifest among us, that God sent his only Son into the world, so that we might live through him. [10] In this is love, not that we loved God but that he loved us and sent his Son to be the expiation for our sins. [11] Beloved, if God so loved us, we also ought to love one another. [12] No man has ever seen God; if we love one another, God abides in us and his love is perfected in us.

13 By this we know that we abide in him and he in us, because he has given us of his own Spirit. [14] And we have seen and testify that the Father has sent his Son as the Savior of the world. [15] Whoever confesses that Jesus is the Son of God, God abides in him, and he in God. [16] So we know and believe the love God has for us. God is love, and he who abides in love abides in God, and God abides in him. [17] In this is love perfected with us, that we may have confidence for the day of judgment, because as he is so are we in this world. [18] There is no fear in love, but perfect love casts out fear. For fear has to do with punishment, and he who fears is not perfected in love. [19] We love, because he first loved us.

RSV

terests that unite friends. You love those with whom you have shared the crises and successes of your life, those who have proved themselves to be dependable, those who have become real friends, tried and true.

This is a costly kind of love. Friends get close to us. They catch glimpses of the "us" that hide behind the masks of social roles. At any moment they can expose us for what we really are. It takes lots of time and energy to have close friends. Friends can make tremendous demands on us.

Yet we need friends. We need their support; we need someone before whom we can unmask and still be accepted; we need to feel that we are important to someone. I think of this kind of love as being peaceful. In *eros* we are seeking something; in *phileo* we are at rest. We enjoy the security of acceptance.

Phileo love is also a God-given capacity. But like *eros* it can be abused. We can draw our circle of friends narrowly and exclude some who need us. We can become complacent and lazy. We can fail to seek the pleasures of new adventures. And we can become so afraid of offending a friend that we lose critical faculty or fail to do what we know should be done.

In contrast with these two loves, there is a third type of love. It aims for the well-being of its object. It motivates the lover to direct his conduct with the loved one toward this goal. The Greeks called this *agape*. This is the kind of love that is identified with the person of God and is evidenced by his actions.

PERSONAL LEARNING ACTIVITY 11
Read the Scripture on the opposite page. Then fill in the blanks below.
1. **The essential nature of God is** _____.
2. **The fact of God's love for us is made evident by**
   _____.
3. **We should respond to God's love by** _____
   _____.
4. **We should fear** _____.
5. **Our loving others is an evidence of** _____
   _____.

Answers are at the end of the chapter.

As we shall see later in the chapter, all the activities of God can be interpreted as evidence of his love. Yet God does not love us in order to have pleasure. He does not need our friendship to enjoy a sense of community. He does seem to appreciate fellowship with us, but within the Trinity there is ample opportunity for fellowship. God does not love us because there is any benefit for him in the relationship.

Listen to Paul's definition of *agape*. It has never been improved upon:

> Love is patient and kind; love is not jealous or boastful; it is not arrogant or rude. Love does not insist on its own way; it is not irritable or resentful; it does not rejoice at wrong, but rejoices in the right. Love bears all things, believes all things, hopes all things, endures all things. Love never ends (1 Cor. 13:4-8, RSV).

God loves us not for what he can get, but rather because it is his nature to give love. The love of God always has amazed believers. The essential paradox of the Christian religion is that our great and good God comes to us in love. Hosea reports the words of God, "I am God and not man, the Holy One in your midst" (11:9). Whereas we may reject those we see as impure, God, the truly pure one, comes to sinful man in love.[1]

What does God give us? He gives us forgiveness and cleansing for the burden of guilt we bear. He gives us acceptance and fellowship. He gives us the promise of eternal life. He provides us with an understanding of history that gives meaning to all of the chaos that surrounds us. He gives us a mission also: we are to share what he has given us with the world.

God is love. The loving God is another distinctive of our religion. This powerful, righteous God encounters us as love. "Amazing Grace! How Sweet the Sound"; "Love Divine, All Loves Excelling"; "Love Lifted Me"; "O Love That Wilt Not Let Me Go"; "The Love of God, How Rich and Pure"—such are the confessions of the faithful. God is love, and we are to love one another even as he has loved us.

However, even as we love with *agape* love, we must be on guard against pride. When we do something unselfish, when we love the unlovely, when we share the gospel, it is so easy for us to become proud of what we have done. This is why we must stay close to God; this is why we must concentrate on the cross; this is why we must listen to the Spirit of God as he comes to convict us of our sinning. Now let us examine how God has made his love manifest in the world; and, therefore, what we mean when we say, "God is love."

THE SCRIPTURES SPEAK OF GOD'S LOVE

In previous chapters I have shown that believers experience God as free, great, and good. This chapter considers God as loving. We see the other side of God's goodness. The acts that demonstrated God's power and righteousness also make his love manifest. The famous verse John 3:16 says something about God's person, work, and will. Since God's nature is love, he sent his Son, he works to redeem humankind, and he wills that we have eternal life.

In the Old Testament

The Hebrews, based on their experiences with God, spoke repeatedly of his loving kindness or mercy (Pss. 86:15; 98:2-3; 103:8-17; 145:8-9; 146:7-9). God helped his people (Pss. 5:7-8; 6:4,8; 18:50; 40:11; 107:6-7). The Hebrews developed a deep sense of relationship with him (Pss. 13:5-6; 31:7; 42:8; 66:20). Psalm 103 is typical of the many psalms that declare the love of God:

> The Lord works vindication and justice for all who are oppressed. He made known his ways to Moses, his acts to the people of Israel. The Lord is merciful and gracious, slow to anger and abounding in steadfast love. He will not always chide, nor will he keep his anger for ever. He does not deal with us according to our sins, nor requite us according to our iniquities. For as the heavens are high above the earth, so great is his steadfast love toward those who fear him; as far as the east is from the west, so far does he remove our transgressions from us. As a father pities his children, so the Lord pities those who fear him. For he knows our frame; he remembers that we are dust. . . . The Lord has established his throne in the heavens, and his kingdom rules over all (Ps. 103:6-19, RSV).

Psalm 103 summarizes much of what is set forth in this book to this point. Listen to its message.

First, we are called on to bless God. To bless is to adore, to worship, to thank. To bless is to respond to acts of love by loving. And why are we to bless God? We are to bless God because of what he has done for us, what he is doing, and what he will do.

We have come to relate the love of God to the acts of creation and maintenance of the universe. Building upon the concept that God is acting redemptively in history, many see creation as God's act to make creatures capable of responding to his love by loving him in return. God's care of the universe is seen also as a manifestation of his love (Job 38:41; Ps. 121:3; Matt. 5:45; 6:26; 10:29).

Second, the psalmist alludes to the roles of King, Judge, and Father that characterize God's relationships with humankind. He "rules over all" (v. 19); "he works vindication and justice" (v. 6); he "pities his children" (v. 13) like a father.

Third, the qualities of freedom, power, justice, and dependability are affirmed. However, the focus of the psalm is on the great love of God. God is merciful and gracious. He is forgiving. His love is dependable, steadfast.

Fourth, God does not play games with us. Through Moses he let the people know what he expected of them. His acts both support his claims to greatness and demonstrate his goodness and love. He reveals his freedom by his treatment of our sins. Although as the good God he takes seriously our sin, as the free, loving God he is not bound to punish us by the letter of the law. He will pardon, redeem, justify, and forgive us. Having experienced this cleansing, having enjoyed the warmth of his love, what can we do but "bless his holy name"?

Certainly the covenants God made with his people show God's love. In them God gives much more than he receives. He gives what we need, and he receives what he might have had by force had he chosen that approach. Likewise his punishment, which had as its intent the redemption of the remnant, was loving. The Exodus, Conquest, Exile, and Restoration can all be interpreted as loving acts of God.

Fifth, the love of God is like a cord that binds his other qualities together in a whole. The free God expresses his freedom in a loving way. The great God uses his power in ways that demonstrate his love. The good God does not allow his holiness to stand in the way of his loving transgressors or his seeking to redeem them.

In the New Testament

Moving to the revelation of God in the period covered by the New Testament, one finds that the love of God is the personality trait which is featured. John had much to say about God's love. He saw love as the essential characteristic of God (1 John 4:16). He saw God's activities of redemption as grounded in love (John 3:16). John recorded how in the shadow of the cross (John 14—17) Jesus spoke long and eloquently about love. Paul said much the same but used the term "grace" (Eph. 2:5-9; 3:14-20; Rom. 5:6-11; 8:34-39). Listen to Paul's interpretation of God's saving activity:

> But God, who is rich in mercy, out of the great love with which he loved us, even when we were dead through our trespasses, made us alive together with Christ (by grace you have been saved), and raised us up with him, and made us sit with him in the heavenly places in Christ Jesus, that in the coming ages he might show the immeasurable riches of his grace in kindness toward us in Christ Jesus (Eph. 2:4-7, RSV).

Certainly it is apparent that Paul conceived of the saving activity of Christ as evidence of God's love.

Paul continued by declaring that God's love is both the cause and the purpose for his giving of the Spirit to dwell within the hearts of believers:

> For this reason I bow my knees before the Father, from whom every family in heaven and on earth is named, that according to the riches of his glory he may grant you to be strengthened with might through his Spirit in the inner man, and that Christ may dwell in your hearts through faith; that you, being rooted and grounded in love, may have power to comprehend with all the saints what is the breadth and length and height and depth, and to know the love of Christ which surpasses knowledge, that you may be filled with all the fulness of God (Eph. 3:14-19, RSV).

Like the psalmist, Paul was compelled to bless and worship the loving God.

In his exposition on "last things," addressed to the Thessalonians, Paul concluded with:

> Now may our Lord Jesus Christ himself, and God our Father, who loved us and gave us eternal comfort and good hope through grace, comfort your hearts and establish them in every good work and word (2 Thess. 2:16-17, RSV).

Apparently Paul saw the coming of Jesus as King and Judge to reward and punish and to establish a just reign as an act of God's love.

For Paul, John, and other disciples the birth, life, death, and resurrection of Jesus, as well as the coming of the Spirit and the return of Christ at the end of time, show the love of God. Love, grace, mercy, kindness—this is the language of the New Testament. Standing as they did at the central moment in history, the disciples were overwhelmed by the love of God.

Love is the characteristic of God that caught their attention and on which their preaching and writing were fixed. It was the love of God that prompted him to send Jesus as our Savior (John 3:16). The writer of Hebrews grounded his long discussion of the purpose of the incarnation in the fact of God's graciousness (Heb. 2:9). Paul did the same. The great, good, free God is known as love. We know this to be true, because his acts reveal love.

PERSONAL LEARNING ACTIVITY 12
Is everything that happens to a Christian the result of God's love for him? Think carefully before answering. Then write out your answer and the reason you believe what you do.

GOD'S ROLES SHOW HIS LOVE

God performs all of his social roles in loving ways. He is a mighty King who treats his subjects with love. He is a righteous Judge whose judgments are tempered by mercy (Ps. 103). But there are several roles that focus specifically on his love.

Shepherd

Shepherd is often used to mean *King*. Although the classic reference for this relationship is Psalm 23, it is used many times elsewhere (Isa. 40:10-11; Ezek. 34:11-12,22-23; John 10:14-18,25-30; Heb. 13:20-21). In Psalm 23 the Shepherd God is pictured as leading. This suggests the subordination of the believer to his Shepherd. The shepherd cared for his sheep in both the good times and the bad times. Note that accepting the lordship of God over your life does not mean that you will not have to deal with evil and suffering. Rather it means that in the face of trouble God will walk before and assist you. The final statement of the psalm is interpreted often as a promise of life eternal.

Kinsman Redeemer
A figure who played a role in Hebrew culture was the *kinsman redeemer* (goel) (Lev. 24:48-49; Ruth 4:1-11). When a Hebrew fell captive or was sold into bondage, his kin were expected to pay for his release. God is pictured as the redeemer of his people, personally and collectively (Job 19:25; Isa. 43:1; 50:1; Jer. 31:29-34; Ezek. 18:4-28).

Husband
Another important figure in Hebrew culture was the *husband* (Jer. 2:2; Ezek. 16:15,32-34; Hos. 2:19-20). The theme of the prophecy of Hosea is that God is a loving husband to Israel. But Israel had proved unfaithful by worshiping other gods. Yet God did not give up on his people. He redeemed them from slavery and restored them to his family. Paul and John used the language of family to depict the relationship between Christ and his church (Rev. 21:2,9; Eph. 5:23).

Father
Of course the key figure is that of God as loving *Father*. The image appears in the Old Testament (Ps. 103:8-17; Hos. 11:1-4); but in the life and teaching of Jesus, *Father* becomes the primary way of referring to God. Certainly the term denotes the unique relationship of Jesus to God. *Father* also is used to indicate the relationship to God of those who have entered into covenant with him (John 14:18-25; 17).

Consider the Sermon on the Mount as an exposition on the role of God as Father. First, Jesus taught that the children of

God are loving people (Matt. 5:44-48). Not only do they love the folk who are nice to them, but those who are not, as well. This is the way God is. This is the way he acts. As his children we are to be like him (Matt. 5:48).

Second, the providential care of the Father is noted (Matt. 6). A recurrent theme is that believers should live their lives to please God, not for the applause of mankind.

Third, our Lord's Model Prayer spells out what our relationship to God ought to be. The opening statement catches both the closeness of our relationship with God and our reverence of him—"Our Father, ... Hallowed be thy name." It continues with an acknowledgment of his sovereignty—"kingdom . . . will be done." Next we recognize our dependence on him—"daily bread." We recognize that he is the model for our lives—"debts . . . debtors." Then we note that even the good we might do is dependent on him—"lead us not . . . deliver us." And the prayer concludes with a statement of adoration (Matt. 6:9-13).

I find thinking about the fatherhood of God in terms of a social role to be helpful. It helps me to focus on the rights and duties of a father, not procreation. What are the rights of a father in relationship with his children? Honor, respect, affection, trust? And what are his obligations? Love, care, support, guidance, assistance? From what we have learned about the nature of God in this study, it is obvious that the qualities of fatherhood describe better than any others the relationship between God and the believer.

This emphasis on the role of loving Father also points up the basic difference between the old and the new covenants. The nature of the old was like that of a legal contract. The nature of the new was like that of a personal relationship. In the new the believer draws near to God. He is drawn by the demonstration of God's sacrificial love in the work of Jesus. God and the believer are united by bonds of love. In a legal relationship it is normal for parties to be primarily concerned with improving their own position. The partner to a contract does what he must do because of the threat of legal action against him if he does not. In a relationship of love, the parties cooperate for their mutual benefit (Heb. 10). The believer does what God wants him to do because of love and respect for the Father.

Suffering Servant

In the role of Suffering Servant, Jesus declared the love of God in a particular way (Isa. 52:13 to 53:12). God is free, great, and good enough that he could lay aside the roles of dominance and become a servant to man. Because he was free he did not have to conform to the traditional understandings about how gods should act. Because he was great he had confidence in his power to win the victory over evil by subjecting himself to its power. Because he was good he would not be satisfied with anything less than victory. Because he was loving he was willing to make this sacrifice, the humiliation and death of his Son.

THE INCARNATION SHOWS HIS LOVE

The incarnation gives evidence to all the qualities of God's person, but it has been customary, and rightly so, to view it primarily as a demonstration of his love. Here as nowhere else are act and person bound together. The act forms the person; the person performs the act. A key passage for comprehending this truth is Philippians 2:1-18. Take time now to read this passage before reading on.

Divine

Paul in agreement with John understood that Jesus was the eternal Son of God, the Word of God, the force by which the universe was made and maintained (1 Cor. 1:15-23; John 1:1-14; 1 John 1:1-4). Paul declared that for Christ to relinquish his position of power and prestige, knowing what awaited him on earth, was an act of great love.

Human

Paul saw Jesus Christ as a human person. The preexistent Christ assumed the limitations of time and space that characterize all humankind. This is borne out by the numerous appeals by Jesus to the authority of the Father and by the fact that Jesus declared his obedience to the Father (John 6: 45-58; 8:41-59; 10:25-30; 12:49-50; 17). The servanthood of Jesus was demonstrated in part by his readiness to meet the people's needs by healing, feeding, touching, forgiving, and teaching truth. Jesus was summarizing the impact of his teachings when in the shadow of the cross he washed the feet of his disciples, hosted a Passover meal, and declared, " 'This is my commandment, that you love one another as I have loved you' " (John 15:12, RSV). Here Jesus purposely assumed the roles of servant and of sacrifice. And with his commandment he set the tone of the ethic of Christianity. His serving, sacrificing love becomes the model for those who call themselves his followers.

However, one must be careful not to confuse servant with servile. Christ is not pictured as a weakling, meekly bowing to the demands of the strong. See him drive the money changers from the Temple (John 2:15). Listen to him condemn the religious authorities (Matt. 23:13-39). There is a great difference between meeting needs, real needs, and being a servile doormat. The former stems from love; the latter, from fear.

Sacrifice
Christ's death as the redemptive sacrifice that made possible the defeat of the forces of evil should be comprehended as an act of love. In many ways the Roman letter is a theology of love. Listen to Paul's interpretation of the cross:

> God shows his love for us in that while we were yet sinners Christ died for us. Since, therefore, we are now justified by his blood, much more shall we be saved by him from the wrath of God. For if while we were enemies we were reconciled to God by the death of his Son, much more, now that we are reconciled, shall we be saved by his life (Rom. 5:8-10, RSV).

And later Paul added:

> No, in all these things we are more than conquerors through him who loved us. For I am sure that neither death, nor life, nor angels, nor principalities, nor things present, nor things to come, nor powers, nor height, nor depth, nor anything else in all creation, will be able to separate us from the love of God in Christ Jesus our Lord (Rom. 8:37-39, RSV).

Plainly, Paul said that the victory is won and love is demonstrated in the cross.

Resurrection

Jesus was raised from the dead and rewarded in heaven for the love he had shown to mankind. He is now serving mankind even further as High Priest (Heb. 7—10). And he is coming again victorious. Vindication, reward, and working out the meaning of love are involved.

PERSONAL LEARNING ACTIVITY 13
The central concept in the Christian ethic is that believers are to become like God. What difference should the fact that God is love make in our personalities, in our relationship with others, and in our activities within the institutions of society?

GOD'S LOVE MAKES COMMUNITY POSSIBLE

God is love.
God so loved the world.
Love one another.
God showed his love . . . Christ died for us.
Who shall separate us from the love of Christ?

Here is what our faith is about. God wills to have community with man. This is the reason why God is pictured as walking in the garden with our ancestors. But they were not willing to accept the fellowship on his terms. They wanted to be his equal. But this was an unrealistic desire. So the community was destroyed. Since then God has worked to restore community with humankind. He knew that community cannot be forced. For true community to evolve in a relationship, partners must choose to participate. Here is the reason why Baptists have championed the concept of liberty of conscience. Believers must want to have fellowship with God; they must be willing to accept the authority of God, his dominance in the relationship; they must be willing to perform the tasks he assigns to them.

The kingdom of God is not a democracy. We do not elect our ruler. We do not make our own laws. The kingdom of God community is a kingship. God is the sovereign. He defines what is right and wrong. He stands ready to naturalize us by forgiving us and cleansing us once we submit ourselves to his sovereignty. But we come on his terms.

Significantly, this invitation is not to be just another subject of the realm. We are invited to be sons, heirs, and joint heirs with Christ. We are the King's kin (Rom. 8:17). This grants us special rights and burdens us with heavy responsibilities. As sons we live in a relationship with the King-Father that is to be characterized by love. Yet we have the tough responsibility of inviting others to join in our community. What has proved still more difficult is the establishment of community among our spiritual brothers and sisters. How far short we fall of loving one another as Jesus loved us. Selfishness, pride, arrogance, pettiness, not to mention the more flagrant sins, are still practiced within the fellowship of most churches. God must really love us to endure our shortcomings.

Early Baptists believed that the church should be a spiritual community. They took seriously the concept that Christians were to love one another as Christ had loved them. Those who presented themselves for membership in a congregation entered into covenant with the other members. Each was to be concerned for the physical and spiritual well-being of the others. Prayer meetings, Bible study, and church discipline were elements of the community. Early Baptists prayed for one another; they searched the Scriptures together; when one fell into sin, they sought to restore that person to the fellowship.[2]

Although there may be less stress on the community concept now than there was then, and although many of our congregations have grown enormously in members, the idea of community is still alive. The sick are visited and prayed for; the bereaved are comforted; the wanderers are sought out. In an age that seems to be seeking community, perhaps this function of the church should be stressed again. We might emphasize how the church does minister to the needs of its members as a support group. We might consider how we can be more effective in this role. We might develop new programs that will build up the fellowship.

However, in all of this we must stress that it is the love of God that is the key. Programs, emphases, and hand-wringing will not do it. True community is grounded in a common thankfulness to the gracious God who loved us, who sacrificed for us, who called us, who forgave and cleansed us. Having had so much done for us, we can understand better the needs and problems of others. Having experienced such a wonderful salvation, we share a common bond with other believers. Through worship and action we grow and share together in our fellowship, maturing in love with one another.

Perhaps the biggest difficulty faced by churches in seeking to become a community is that many of us are satisfied with ourselves. We have lost sight of the truth of the early Baptist John Bunyan, who saw the Christian life as a pilgrimage.[3] We feel as if we arrived when we were saved. Instead we must see that conversion is only the arrival at the beginning point. The journey is still ahead. By making it with a group of other pilgrims we can share the successes, offer support, and grow as we go.[4]

PERSONAL LEARNING ACTIVITY 14
See if you can answer the following questions with one sentence for each answer. Why does God will community for man? How is love essential to the relationship of community? Now list specific reasons you do or do not feel a sense of community in your church.

CONCLUSION

God is love. A short sentence, but one full of significance. Having looked at four basic characteristics of God in a kind of chronological order—free (eternal spirit), great (creation), good (covenant), love (incarnation), now let me reverse the process and consider God from the perspective of the believer.

Most believers have their initial encounter with God in a moment when his love is most evident. The event may have occurred because of awareness that God is great or good, but at the moment it is the love of God that is most evident. When God became real to me, I was scared of his power and his judgment; it was his love that conquered me and drew me to him. Only then do we begin to comprehend his goodness, his greatness, and his freedom. The better we come to know God, the more wonderful his love becomes. The same is true of his other qualities.

It is important to speak of God as a person and to see his qualities of personality in terms of their relationship with the person. We know God as free, great, good, and loving in our experiences with him. God is not an object that must fit into philosophical categories. He is a person and is most fully known as such. The qualities of his personality are not subject to proof. They are known in encounter.[5]

For example, as I reflect on the acts of my father, I see them as good and loving. When he was punishing me for some misconduct, I might not have so defined the act. But from the distance of time and experience with others, I have come to define my father as essentially a good and loving person.

In interpersonal relations we walk by faith, not the facts of logic. Based on what I have experienced, plus what someone says about himself, plus what others say about him, I develop a definition of a person's character. I may be wrong; others may be wrong; and the person may be fooling us. But I operate on my definition of the character of my partner in encounter. Having defined my father as good and loving, I acted toward him accordingly.

God has told us that he is free, great, good, loving. Others have stated that this is true. His acts declare this. We have experienced this. We do not always understand what God is doing. Sometimes we may question his actions. They may not seem appropriate in terms of the way we understand his character and/or the situation. Hang on. Let us recheck our definitions and our understanding. Many people have known God for a long time. The evidence is in his favor. He is great, good, loving, free.

Another warning should be sounded. Some believers have stressed one facet of God's character and neglected the others. Some have focused almost exclusively on God's love while others have neglected the love of God in their heavy emphasis on the role of God as Judge. He is both: love and Judge—and King as well.

One of the most difficult tasks people face is to manage their several and diverse roles. For example, while preparing this text, I have experienced tension from the difficulties of managing my roles of father, professor, minister, and writer. Because of the expectations and responsibilities that come with each of these roles, I have not been able temporarily to measure up to any of them. The audiences for each role have not allowed me to separate these roles.

I wonder if some of the problems we have in understanding

God result from the fact that we expect him to come in one role, but he may come in another. I wonder if sometimes we will not allow him to separate his roles. Specifically, how can God be King, Judge, and Father at the same time for every person?

At our church we like to sing "I'm a child of the king." That is what the love of God is about. In salvation we become children of the King with all the rights, privileges, responsibilities, and duties. Think about it. Isn't this wonderful?

Answers to Personal Learning Activity 11
1. love
2. the coming of Jesus to save us
3. loving him and our fellows
4. nothing
5. our salvation and our new relationship to God

NOTES

1. There are several good studies available on God's love. A basic reference that approaches this subject from a historical perspective is Anders Nygren's *Agape and Eros*, tr. by Philip S. Watson (Philadelphia: The Westminster Press, 1953). C. S. Lewis presents a helpful analysis in *The Four Loves* (New York: Harcourt Brace Jovanovich, Inc., 1960). Wisely, Walter Thomas Conner, in *Revelation and God*, pp. 253-54, stated that God's love is not something to define; rather, it is to be described (Nashville: Broadman Press, 1936).

2. For some insight into what Baptists have believed across the years about the function of the church, one might consult Duke K. McCall, ed., *What Is the Church?* (Nashville: Broadman Press, 1958).

3. One of the classics of Christian devotional literature is *The Pilgrim's Progress*. It speaks in the language of allegory of the Christian's life being a journey toward the heavenly city. It was written by John Bunyan, a seventeenth-century tinker-minister of the General Baptist persuasion.

4. Walter T. Conner makes the point that the Christian life is one of growth toward maturity, in *The Gospel of Redemption*, pp. 139-45, 258-68 (Nashville: Broadman Press, 1945).

5. A book that has shaped my thinking about the subject of how we know God is Emil Brunner's *Truth as Encounter* (Philadelphia: The Westminster Press, 1964).

Chapter 5

"My God Is Real"

A basic teaching of the Christian faith is that God is person. I know my God is real because we have communicated. God must not be merely a doctrine, an object to be studied. God is a person, and to be known he must be encountered.

We had some good times at our Saturday night Baptist Student Union meetings in Kansas City in the 1950's. Our leader, Anderine Farmer, was a creative person. We enjoyed singing, Bible study, and various social action events; but mostly we enjoyed one another. In the fall of 1958 several student nurses from General Hospital joined our group. I was unusually impressed with one of their number. She was tall, pretty, and smiled a lot. She was bright, a leader among the student nurses. I saw in her a lot of the qualities I valued.

After the meetings many of us would go to Roy and Ray's, a drive-in just off the Plaza, for onion rings and other fattening foods. Our group would crowd into a corner booth and tease and laugh as we ate. There I got better acquainted with Jackie, and what I learned confirmed my earlier evaluation.

Fearing rejection, I proceeded cautiously. Several months passed, and I was more certain what the answer would be before I asked her for a date. I was quite concerned that I present the right image—interested, but not too much so. She admitted later that she felt the same. At first we were self-conscious. We talked about the things youth talked about then—classes, favorite television shows, pet peeves, amusing experiences, successes, goals for the future. We went places together—plays, church, ball games, picnics, and the like. Gradually we became more relaxed, open, and honest in each other's presence. Building on the initial attraction bonds, we added bonds of shared experiences, of shared values, of shared expectations. We were good for each other. It was wonderful to know that someone important to each of us liked, accepted, and encouraged the other.

In the process of courtship we both changed. The processes of seeking acceptance, of being concerned for someone other than oneself, of sharing one's inner being, caused growth. After several months it seemed to me that the benefits of continuing a relationship with Jackie were greater than the costs. I began to do and say things that were intended to give her the opportunity to say she felt the same about our relationship. When we knew our feelings were the same, we moved to a more serious level in our courtship.

We both realized the importance of the life commitment of marriage. We knew that our whole lives would be affected seriously by this choice. We alternately tested and trusted the other's sincerity. Sometimes we had doubts. But as the relationship continued, it grew in depth, in intensity, and in meaning.

Through our courtship and in marriage, more and more of ourselves came to be encompassed by our relationship. In the beginning we had been concerned primarily with the immediate goals of enjoying ourselves. With our commitment to a life together, we became more concerned with long-range goals of building bonds that would provide a basis for a lasting relationship. We planned for the future together. Both of us have had to make adjustments. We have become increasingly honest in expressing our expectations for each other and in our evaluation of each other.[1]

The courtship of Jackie and Gary is by no means unique. Many other couples have had similar experiences. There are a number of important concepts dealing with the development of relationships between people. These concepts can be used to understand what happened between Jackie and Gary, and the relationship that emerged between them. They can be used also to understand the gospel.

A basic teaching of the Christian faith is that God is person. I know my God is real because we have communicated. The basic idea of *The Doctrine of God* is that God must not be merely a doctrine, an object to be studied. God is a person, and to be known he must be encountered. The life of the Christian is to be a process of repeated encounters with God. Through these meetings, as in a courtship and marriage, a re-

lationship grows and matures. Does the Bible not speak of
Israel as the wife of God (Hos.) and of the church as the
bride of Christ (Rev. 21:2-9)? This was no accident. The
writers knew the importance of developing a relationship.

The first four chapters of *The Doctrine of God* have presented
some of the basic characteristics of God's person. Here I want
to draw these together in a definition of *person*. I will look at
how God is uniquely person. Then I will suggest how God acts
and is known as a person. I will draw upon the insights of the
social sciences, and I will use my experiences in our family as
examples of how relationships develop.

MEANING OF PERSONHOOD: ESSENTIAL ELEMENTS
As we know persons, they are made up essentially of body,
mind, conscience, and will. The term *spirit* is often used to refer
to mind, conscience, and will.

A Person Has a Body
As *bodies*, persons experience the limitations of space and time.
Bodies are located in specific space, and they experience
change through time. Apparently bodies have certain needs or
drives including basic maintenance functions and perhaps such
psychological needs as the need for affection and the need for
new experiences. Bodies also have the senses—sight, hearing,
feel, taste, and touch—which they use to perceive their sur-
roundings.

A Person Has a Mind
The normal *mind* has the capacity for memory and recall. A
person uses this power to remember and recall in order to
interpret and understand what is happening at the moment
and to decide how to respond. Also, a person uses his mind to
plan for the future. Most persons like to exercise some control
over the future. They do this by using their minds to think
ahead and plan. When I decided I was in love with Jackie and
wanted to marry her, I set about to achieve that goal. I planned
my strategy; I was careful about what I did and said; I considered the probable results of my actions toward her. Based
on what I had learned and observed about person-to-person relationships, I moved cautiously toward my goal. As I moved
toward my goal, my mind was very sensitive to her responses

to my actions. I continually was modifying my conduct and reevaluating my goal as our courtship progressed. This illustrates the way a person uses his mind not only to understand what is happening at the present but also to plan for and to influence what happens in the future.

A Person Has a Conscience
Closely related to the mind is the *conscience*. As we grow up we are taught what is right and what is wrong. Christians believe that the Holy Spirit informs the conscience of a believer. It is the conscience that leads a person in his evaluation of his plans, his conduct, the conduct of others, and his responses to his everyday experiences.

A Person Has a Will
The *will* is the ability a person has to follow through on his plans and to react effectively to the demands of everyday life. Because a person has a will, he is able not only to make choices, determine goals, and set aims but also to take whatever actions and to make whatever sacrifices may be necessary to achieve those goals and aims.[2]

MEANING OF PERSONHOOD: SOCIAL ELEMENTS
There is far more to personhood than the essential elements of body, mind, conscience, and will. Persons are essentially social beings. The exciting part of being a person is encounter with other persons.

Indirect Encounter
One way we encounter persons is through the products of their activity. When one reads great literature, listens to great music, or looks at great art, he often wonders about the person who created it. Biographies of great persons are popular because we like to try to understand why those persons became great, and what experiences stimulated their creativity.

Person-to-Person Encounters
Although indirect encounters can be significant, the kind of encounter I want to focus on is face-to-face encounter. By this I

mean the direct relationship between persons. It is important for us to understand several things about person-to-person encounter if we are to understand our relationship with God.

We encounter others for various purposes.—Some of these are purely instrumental. For example, when I hire a plumber, I am interested in his skills, not the compatibility of our personalities. Other face-to-face encounters are expressive. Here the concern is with compatibility of personalities; skills are secondary. Most relationships involve both types; and when an instrumental relationship is repeated, there is a tendency for expressive elements to emerge.

The growth of a relationship is determined by certain factors.—These factors are place, occasion, rules of morality and etiquette, social roles in play, and whether one has encountered the person before. Where this meeting occurs, the nature of the occasion, what society defines as appropriate behavior, and the social role you are playing affect how you act toward the person you encounter. The same is true of how the other person responds to your behavior.

Person-to-person encounters produce knowledge.—We learn through interaction. Generally, we learn about the processes of sociability. We learn how social roles can be played. We learn strategies for achieving our goals. Specifically we learn some things about particular persons. And by getting to know others we, by reflection, come to know ourselves more fully.

Generally, there are three kinds of knowledge we gather in person-to-person encounter: knowledge about how people act, knowledge of other selves, knowledge of ourselves. All three kinds are valuable.

The self grows through person-to-person encounter.—We are a part of everyone, or at least of many of the ones, we have met. In encounter I present an image of myself. My partner responds to this self. He or she likes it, dislikes it, or could care less. I also indicate my understanding and purposes in the encounter. My partner responds to me and to what I am doing. I use that response to check the effectiveness of what I am doing. If I think the other person has not understood my actions or seen me as I intended to be seen, I may try again. I may change my approach, or I may withdraw from the encounter. In any case, my success or failure in the encounter may cause me to rethink who I really am and how I stand in relationship to others.

The relationship affects the persons participating in it.—In time a relationship becomes something in itself. Important bonds are developed. Maintenance of the relationship becomes important. To become involved in a relationship with another person puts restraints on both persons. Friends and family are costly. Time and energy that could be expended in seeking personal goals are diverted to maintenance of the relationship. One may have to forego personal desires and goals for the good of the group. He may have to meet needs of those he loves before meeting his own needs. But relationships also bring benefits. And most of us seem to feel that the benefits outweigh the costs.

A person, then, is a unique being who encounters other beings. Among the beings who may encounter another being is the dominant personage, God. I want to use this foundation of concepts about personality and relationships between persons to construct a fuller understanding of the Christian belief that God is person. The sections that follow will deal with these three faith affirmations: (1) God is a whole person. (2) God interacts with humankind in relationships, and one knows him most fully within these encounters. (3) Feedback from our relationship with God has an impact on our personality.

GOD IS PERSON

God is spiritual person; we are fleshly. The fact that Jesus had to empty himself to become like us indicates that God's personhood is vastly superior to ours. Yet we are taught by the Scriptures that man was created in the image of God. Certainly "image" involves personhood.[3] The language used to describe God is the language of personhood. What can be said about God's personhood? If we build on the definition of *person* developed early in this chapter, several things can be said.

The Four Elements of Personhood Can Be Linked with the Four Qualities of God

Earlier we saw that a person is a being who has body, mind, conscience, and will and who is conscious of self as distinguished from other selves. He is able to interact with other personages. These four elements of person link with the four qualities of God (great, good, free, loving) presented in the previous chapters.

Great/Will.—If one acknowledges the greatness of God, it is not difficult for him to see God as one who has made choices, determined goals, and established aims. "Thy will be done" (Matt. 6:10). Again, Christ's prayer in the garden, "Not my will, but thine, be done" (Luke 22:42). The Christian life is pictured as being one committed to doing God's will.

Good/Conscience.—Again, if one acknowledges the goodness of God, it follows that he has a conscience. To speak of God as just and righteous, as the Bible does, is to assume that God has a conscience.

Free/Mind.—Jesus once said, " 'You will know the truth and the truth will make you free' " (John 8:32, RSV). Freedom and truth are integrally related. Real truth is from God. Truth is something grasped by the mind. Thus the free God, who makes us free through knowledge of his truth, must have a mind.

Love/Body or Form.—Although *agape* love is more action than emotion, it is action that results from an emotion or a feeling. The seat of a person's emotions or feelings is his form. In man, this is his physical body. Since God is a person who has emotions and feelings, he must have form or substance or being in which those emotions and feelings reside and through which they are expressed. At the same time we know that this form is not a body like our bodies, and we should carefully avoid thinking of God in physical terms. To have form or substance or being does not mean he is necessarily subject to the limitations of the physical body, and we should not think of God in such terms. An example of this is Christ's form after his resurrection. He was not limited by time and space. I suppose that at least since my days in Mrs. Button's Primary Sunday School department, I have wondered what God looked like. I still do not know.

Form is a rich concept. To speak of form or substance or being is to speak of more than the physical body. It is to speak of sentiments, emotions, and senses. In man it is the body (our form) that makes possible our awareness of what is around us. It is the body (our form) that provides us with the facilities to respond to our environment. There are numerous accounts in the Scriptures that show that God experiences and expresses feelings and emotions, that he is aware of things, and that he acts upon his creation (Pss. 89:13; 44:24; 37:24). Because God is aware and feels and acts, we know he has form.

PERSONAL LEARNING ACTIVITY 15
Rethink what the author said about God having form. Write out what you understand to be the distinction between having form and having *a body*. Do you agree with the author that God has form? Write out the reasons you agree or disagree.

God Is a Super Person
God's personhood is in every way greater than human personality. His body and mind are not limited by flesh and form, nor by time and space. Traditional theology states that God knows all the past, present, and the future. His conscience is fully developed. It is he who defines the right and the good. His will has both the power and the capacity to achieve his ends.

God Is a Whole Person
God is not immature or incomplete. God knows who he is and where he is headed.

Some may object to the fact that God is called *he* rather than *she* or *it*. They miss the point. God is called *he* because God is functioning in roles normally occupied by males. However, his character and actions include functions that are normally ascribed to females in Western cultures—creativity, love, mercy, compassion. God is a whole person. He gathers up in his personality the best characteristics of both males and females.[4]

PERSONAL LEARNING ACTIVITY 16
What is your reaction to the idea that God's person includes female personality qualities? React to this statement: When considering the qualities of God's personhood, it is better to say that he is both male and female rather than to say that he is neither male nor female.

ENCOUNTERING GOD AS A PERSON

For many centuries it was popular in theology to develop logical proofs of the existence of God. It followed that if one could prove God's existence, then people should believe in him. But some delighted in disproving the proofs, thereby raising questions about God's being and about whether a person should believe in God. However, this was to miss the essential point of Christian faith. God is not an object that can be subjected to logical proofs. God is a person to be known in and through encounters. Further, the knowledge of encounters is a special kind of knowledge. It always involves an element of faith in the trustworthiness of the person known.

God Has a Name

When God decided it was time to call his children out of Egypt, he appeared to Moses and announced to him his name: YHWH (pronounced Jehovah). He said that he had been known to Abraham and his heirs as God Almighty (El Shaddai) (Ex. 6:1-4). Names were important to the Hebrews since they described the character of the bearer. Abraham needed to know that God was almighty if he were to accept the covenant God offered. YHWH has as its root meaning, being. Its essential meaning may be " 'I am who I am' " (Ex. 3:14, RSV). God is the personal being who is making himself known to his people. How? As all people are known—by what they do, by what they say, by the way the persons they encounter interpret what they say and do. One might summarize the biblical account by saying that YHWH, the creator, redeemer, and perfecter of existence, is revealing himself to mankind through his acts and words because this knowledge of his person is an essential element in the accomplishment of his purposes. And yet as a person there always remains unrevealed transcendent qualities of his personhood.

PERSONAL LEARNING ACTIVITY 17
Of the many names used for God in the Bible, which is your favorite? Take time to consider the reasons this is your favorite name for God? What does it say about your relationship with God? What does it say about what you have been taught about God?

God and Social Roles

God meets us in his several roles. He comes as King, Judge, Father, and Suffering Servant. Each role has task (instrumental) elements. Each role has rights and obligations attached to it. In three of these roles God is dominant. In the fourth he becomes subservient to achieve his goal of redemption. The fact that God relates to us in many different roles can make things difficult for us. We want him always to be loving Father, even when we sin. But if we are not repentant, he may encounter us as righteous Judge. We may focus on one facet of God's personality, as revealed in his roles, and neglect the others.

God's Acts and the Needs of the Context

God meets us where we are. This means that he meets our needs, that he accommodates himself to our ability to comprehend him, and that when possible he operates within the limits of the situation at the time and the people's concept of him. For example, in the early days of the Hebrew nation, God was known as War Lord. At that moment the people needed that kind of God. This was the kind of god other nations claimed to have. This is the kind of expectation the Hebrews had for a God. Only gradually did he make himself known as a moral God, as loving, and as Suffering Servant. God moved step by step. He knew that to achieve his long-range goals he must wait until some of the people were ready to understand. Many did not. But there were always a few who were able to move on to a fuller comprehension of the person of God.

God's Acts and the Maturity of His People

Further, God accommodated his will for the people to their degree of readiness to follow it. In the Old Testament God dealt with his people through a covenant of law. Since Christ we relate to God in terms of a covenant of grace. In the Sermon on the Mount, Jesus taught that God demanded more than the law called for (Matt. 5:17-48). Elsewhere he taught that Moses allowed for divorce because of the people's " 'hardness of heart' " (Matt. 19:8-9, RSV).

Although God acknowledges our expectations in an encounter, he teaches better expectations; although he acknowledges our definition of the situation, he gives us a more adequate one; although he accepts our roles, he offers us better ones. Consider Jesus' encounter with his disciples at Caesarea Philippi. When Peter affirmed that Jesus was the Christ and Jesus acknowledged this, it seemed to adjust their relationship. Jesus assumed this role. And he gave to the disciples a new role with certain rights and duties attached. Jesus waited to do this until they were ready and the setting was right (Matt. 16: 13-20).

Learning Through Encounter

In encounter with God we learn. Essentially it is knowledge about his person and our person and about his will and our will. The goal of religious knowledge is to understand the will of God for his universe, and specifically his will for me. It is to understand the person of God. In turn, I come to understand myself better and to assume roles and styles of performance that are in accord with his will. In establishing a relationship with us, God demands to become our significant other. We are to please him before any other—even ourselves (1 Thess. 4:1). As the relationship progresses the meaning of this demand expands.

God's Purposes

God has both instrumental and expressive purposes in mind as he encounters us. So do we. God has tasks for his children. He calls us to do things that are of service to his goals for his creation. These may be tasks within the program of the church. These may be tasks within community organizations. These may be tasks within the home. Further, he wants us to accept his dominance in the roles of King, Judge, and Father over our lives. He also wants us to accept his role of Suffering Servant. By so doing we experience the joy of God's expressive function, his love; and we share his love with others.

PERSONAL LEARNING ACTIVITY 18
Take time to think and identify one instrumental

purpose and one expressive purpose you feel God has for your life. Now list the things you and God are doing to see that those purposes are realized.

Costs and Benefits

What about costs and benefits? God's grace costs him a lot. It costs him the anguish brought about by our rebellion and lack of appreciation. It costs him continuing struggle with the force of evil. It even cost him his Son. His benefits come now as we repent, accept his dominance, and receive his love. His ultimate benefits come when his will is done perfectly and everyone confesses that he is Lord at the end of time. The encounter with God is costly to us. It can end our self-satisfaction. It can make us aware of how inferior we are. But the real benefits outweigh the costs. It is not easy for us to acknowledge our subordination to anyone. But the experience of God's love and the hope of glory are well worth the cost.

God to Be Known as Person

Knowledge of persons is a special kind of knowledge. Religion is not to prove God exists, but it is to come to know him personally. Persons are harder to know than things. This is because persons decide and act. We can know them only by what they say and what they do. We can never possess and control them. They might be fooling us, and we might be misunderstanding them. Risk and faith are involved. I have stressed that God is known in the roles of Suffering Servant, mighty King, righteous Judge, and loving Father. Through these roles, their related acts, and his self-affirmations believers have learned that God is free, great, good, and loving.

The free God comes when, where, and how he wills. The experience of many believers has been that he comes more often when people have prepared themselves to meet him. Bible study, prayer, worship, confession, and contemplation are activities that prepare the heart for the coming of God. The crises of life, when the adequacy of one's world view is called into question, are used frequently by God to encounter persons. For nonbelievers I would suggest the same. Open yourself to an encounter with God. Study the Bible, confess your sins, ask him to come to you. And when crises come, see if the Christian world view does not provide an adequate understanding.

PRACTICING THE PRESENCE OF GOD

In the history of Christianity some believers have been embarrassed by the thought that God is personal. They have preferred to think about God in more impersonal terms such as "over soul" or "ground of being." Most Baptists have believed that the personal Spirit of God convicts sinners of their transgressions; that he comes with the experience of saving grace to cleanse and renew the new believer; that he becomes an ever present inner presence in the life of the believer, empowering, guiding, comforting, and keeping.

This view is rooted in the biblical revelation. Paul spoke forcefully of Christ's being in us and our being in him (Rom. 8). John wrote of communion with the risen Christ (Rev. 3:20).

Baptists like to sing about the personal presence of God in their lives. "My God Is Real," "Breathe on Me," "What a Friend We Have in Jesus," "Sweet Hour of Prayer," and "Near to the Heart of God" are among our favorites. According to the Stark and Glock survey results, 80 percent of Southern Baptists were certain that as adults they had experienced the real presence of God. An additional 14 percent thought that they had. This was a higher percentage than the responses from the members of any other denomination questioned in their study.[5]

Yet in my discussion with ministers, I find a common complaint is that so few of the members of their congregation take seriously the concept that the Spirit of God is a living presence in their lives. Certainly they experienced the presence of God at conversion and perhaps in some of the crises in their lives. But he is not real for them on the job, in the kitchen, on the sports field, at play, or in the classroom. For them the Spirit of God comes and goes; he is not an abiding presence.

CONCLUSION

This chapter should have deepened your understanding of God as a person. To explore adequately the thoughts outlined herein a whole book is needed. Perhaps I have been successful in calling your attention to the key points: (1) God is known as a person, not a thing. (2) Knowledge of persons is different from knowledge of things. (3) Knowledge of other persons has an impact upon ourselves. (4) Knowledge of others shapes our relationships with them. (5) The importance of significant others carries over into other relations. (6) There is a growth factor in a continuing relationship.

In this chapter I have attempted to indicate how all the material in this book to this point can be tied together. The qualities of God's personhood are freedom, greatness, goodness, and love. The person of the God we meet is characterized by these qualities. We know this not only through the testimony of the Scriptures and of others but also by your own experience of God as well. This is the reason that the concept of the Christian life, walking in the way with God, is so important. Essentially, being a Christian is getting to know God more fully and more deeply. This has an impact on our personality. We become more like him.

NOTES

1. Since becoming a student of sociology, I realize how important this process is. Much conflict between people will be resolved if two things happen. First, they need to work out common goals and means of achieving these goals. Second, they need to be aware of and share the expectations they have for themselves and for each other. By expectations I mean such things as treatment of each other, treatment of friends and kin, setting of priorities, and conduct or life-style in general. Of course, the key to all of this is the involved persons' commitment to making the relationship work, and this commitment is expressed through integrity in the treatment of each other.

2. Reinhold Niebuhr develops these categories in the first section of *The Self and the Dramas of History* (New York: Charles Scribner's Sons, 1956). This is an important book for those who would bring the insights of the social sciences upon theology.

3. Emil Brunner develops this idea extensively in *Man in Revolt* (Philadelphia: The Westminster Press, 1947). Compare Emil Brunner, *The Christian Doctrine of Creation and Redemption, Dogmatics: Vol. II* (Philadelphia: The Westminster Press, 1952).

4. Based on Jeremiah 31:21-22 one could contend that Israel is the consort of God. The idea that God has both male and female qualities is similar to the concept current in the women's liberation movement called androgynous.

5. Rodney Stark and Charles Y. Glock, *American Piety* (Berkeley and Los Angeles: University of California Press, 1968), pp. 125-40.

Chapter 6

"In the Name of the Father . . ."

When I was a small boy, I had a problem with the Doxology because of the reference to the Holy Ghost. Based on the information I had gleaned from the stories told to me by my older cousins there were no ghosts who merited the descriptive adjective "holy."

A little later I learned that the Doxology was a theological affirmation of the doctrine of the Trinity. This doctrine says that we worship one God, but he is known as three persons —Father, Son, and Ghost or Spirit. Although the three are distinct in function, they are the same in essence of being. Now that set my fertile imagination to working overtime. It also gave my young Jewish friends and me something to argue about while we waited for the bus after school.

I imagine that I heard most of the illustrations we like to use to explain the Trinity: the three states of water—liquid, solid, and steam; the three parts of an egg; and even 3-in-1 oil. I would find some comfort in first one then another of these. Then some irreverent person would challenge the analogy —the same water cannot be all three at the same time—and I would be off again.

As a seminary student I learned that through the ages the doctrine of the Trinity had been a difficult one for the scholars of the church. It was argued for centuries before the scholars could agree on a statement.[1] Further, I learned that in our own nation about two hundred years ago the doctrine was challenged for not conforming to the canons of logic. Many rejected it. Out of this debate came the Unitarian denomination.

It appeared that the relationship of the Son to the other two persons was particularly problematic for the church scholars. One might believe in a fatherly God. One might have no difficulty believing his Spirit can be present among believers while

God is in heaven. But where does the Son fit in? How can someone be eternally begotten. How could Jesus be fully human and fully divine?[2] How could God be in the flesh, yet be in heaven? Honest theologians seldom have been fully satisfied, intellectually, with their answers to these and related questions. It is impossible for us to stop thinking mathematically. Logic pushes either toward one or three. Here again we must not allow ourselves to be ruled by logic. We must learn to live with that which breaks the bounds and goes beyond our capacity to understand, yet is experienced as true.

MEANING OF TRINITY

The following ideas have helped me. I offer them to those of you who have struggled with this doctrine as help from one pilgrim to another.

The Doctrine of the Trinity Is a Functional Doctrine

The doctrine of the Trinity does the job of explaining the experience of the church with God. In the New Testament God made himself known as Father, Son, and Spirit. On some occasions, for example the baptism of Jesus, all three were present at the same time (Matt. 3:13-17). Jesus commanded that converts be baptized in the name of each of these (Matt. 28:19-20). Jesus claimed to be the Son of God (John 10:30). He promised that the Spirit would come (John 14:15-27). He stated that he is one with the Father (John 10:30). The writer of Hebrews pictured Jesus acting as our High Priest before God (Heb. 7—10). Elsewhere Jesus is pictured as triumphant King, handing the redeemed creation over to his Father (1 Cor. 15:24-28). The early Christians were accused of worshiping three gods. But they would not allow this. Christians said they worshiped one God, yet that God is known in three persons.

It appears that the early church did not worry much about how three could be one. They simply reported their experience. As difficult as it may be for us to see it logically, the doctrine of the Trinity works well to summarize the belief and experience of the early church.

God Is Spirit

Our direct knowledge is of the physical. Spirit is of a different nature, quality, dimension—a different kind of reality. We know, for example, that the spiritual is not limited by time and space, as is the physical. Recall how the resurrected body of Jesus was able to appear and disappear, alternately to be recognized and unrecognized, to have substance and partake of physical food, yet pass through locked doors, to rise into heaven (Luke 24:1-43; John 21:1-23).

Thus, although it may not seem possible for three persons to be one within the physical world with which we are acquainted, can we say that this would not be possible in the spiritual realm? No. In our limited experience with the spiritual, we can see that it is not limited by the laws that regulate the physical universe. So we should not deny the possibility of the Trinity on the basis of the physical impossibility of it.

God Is Person

I have previously shown that personality is not limited by the canons of logic. Even in the realm of the physical one plays many different roles. I am husband, father, teacher, politician, preacher, son, and so forth. Of course I play all these roles through one body, and normally I play them one at a time. But we know that God as Spirit is present everywhere. We know that he can be intensely, personally present in the hearts of millions of people all at the same time. So why cannot we imagine that he as spiritual person can function as three persons (roles) all at the same time while being only one in essence?

The fact that none of the great theologians of the church have expressed the doctrine of the Trinity in a way wholly satisfactory to all believers is comforting. I should not expect to succeed where the great minds have failed. It is of benefit to study their efforts. For in the final analysis the arguments come back to an affirmation of faith.

I particularly appreciate the emphasis of Henry Van Dusen. He suggests that we have formulated the doctrine backward. In reality, we come to know God as Spirit, then as Son, and finally as Father. God comes to us first as convictor of sins, then as Savior, and only then as Lord. In this argument we come full circle. God encounters us in three different ways, roles, personages. Yet God is essentially the same person in all three manifestations.[3]

OVERVIEW

In the final analysis, for me, the doctrine of the Trinity is not something to be proved or disproved. It is rather a useful statement of faith that affirms some things about God which, as we shall see, are very basic. Let us, then, direct our attention to what Baptists have said about the Trinity. Our source will be the statements or confessions of faith.

In the first chapter I noted that Baptists are not a creedal people. God is our Lord. His will is our authority. The Scriptures are the record of God's revelation in words and deeds to his people. God's Spirit helps us to understand the meaning of the Scriptures and to apply their truths to our present life situation. Primarily for the purposes of explaining to non-Baptists what we believe and as an aid in instructing converts concerning what most Baptists have believed, many confessions of faith have been framed by various Baptist bodies across the years. In the Introduction I cited some of the most significant ones.

In the intervening chapters I have searched the Scriptures to learn what they teach about the nature, work, and will of God. Now, against this background we are prepared to give our attention to what the statements or confessions of faith, as formal statements of faith, affirm about God. Specifically, we are interested in the concept of the Trinity. Our focus will fall on the most recent statement, "The Baptist Faith and Message," adopted by messengers to the annual meeting of the Southern Baptist Convention, in Kansas City, Missouri, in 1963.[4]

Do not think I am a creedalist. I am not. But I realize the statements or confessions can be valuable tools for expanding our understanding of our faith. They can help believers by showing them what others, whom we see as brothers, have believed. They help us by furnishing bench marks for our personal understanding of the faith.

The doctrine of God has not been a point of significant contention among Baptists. As I shall show, Baptists have agreed about the nature of God, the Trinity and its three persons. Some disagreements have occurred in interpreting his work, but these must be left for the most part to other studies.

The statement on God in "The Baptist Faith and Message," in my opinion, is the best organized of the Baptist confessions.

It begins with a basic statement of the nature of the Trinity. It then looks in turn at each member of the Trinity, noting the biblical teaching concerning the nature and work of each.

Trinity

> There is one and only one living and true God. He is an intelligent, spiritual, and personal Being, the Creator, Redeemer, Preserver, and Ruler of the universe. God is infinite in holiness and all other perfections. To Him we owe the highest love, reverence, and obedience. The eternal God reveals Himself to us as Father, Son, and Holy Spirit, with distinct personal attributes, but without division of nature, essence, or being.[5]

This statement repeats the 1925 statement with only minor modifications.[6] Sentences are shortened. Redeemer is inserted. And "the eternal God" replaces "he is." This in turn is essentially a restatement of the New Hampshire Confession, 1833.[7] And it in turn seems to be an abbreviated form of the earlier statement on the "Holy Trinity," appearing in the Philadelphia Confession, 1742, formulated in the technical language of scholastic Calvinism. It contains a statement of God's freedom, stressing that he is Lord and is not dependent on anyone or anything. Then it offers a statement on the Trinity:

> In this divine and infinite Being there are three subsistences, the Father the Word (or Son) and Holy Spirit, of one substance, power, and Eternity, each having the whole Divine Essence, yet the Essence undivided, the Father is of none neither begotten nor proceeding, the Son is Eternally begotten of the Father, the holy Spirit proceeding from the Father and the Son, all infinite, without beginning, therefore but one God, who is not to be divided in nature and Being; but distinguished by several peculiar, relative properties, and personal relations; which doctrine of the Trinity is the foundation of all our Communion with God, and comfortable dependence on him.

Behind this statement lies centuries of theological debates as learned scholars have sought to express the nature of the Trinity in a way acceptable to philosophical categories current in their day. Although much less exact, our modern statements and confessions seem to allow God to appear more personal and personable. Yet something of his freedom, majesty, and incomprehensibleness is lost.

What can we say about the content of these statements?—They all hold forth one God. They say something about the greatness, goodness, and love of God. They all hold forth the Trinity. The briefer, modern statement of the Trinity is expressed in nontechnical language, although the earliest confession summarizes the consensus of scholastic theology.

What, specifically, do the confessions affirm about the Trinity?—First, there is essential unity among the persons—"without division of nature, essence, or being." The Father, Son, and Spirit are spirit beings, with shared world view, values, attitudes, goals, and purposes. They share a common self. Essence refers to the basic qualities of something. Second, the Father, Son, and Spirit are distinct in manifestation and function. Third, there is a sense of unity and of community that bonds the three into one. This is the best we can do. The how of the Trinity remains wrapped in mystery because our knowledge of spiritual reality is so limited.

PERSONAL LEARNING ACTIVITY 19
Spend some time thinking about the Trinity. How would you explain the idea that God is one, yet three? Can you express this in logical language?

God the Father

"The Baptist Faith and Message" statement proceeds beyond the 1925 and the New Hampshire statements in elaborating on the nature and work of the persons of the Trinity. In this, the statement follows the practice of the seventeenth-century confessions.

> God as Father reigns with providential care over His universe, His creatures, and the flow of the stream of human history according to the purposes of His grace. He is all powerful, all loving, and all wise. God is Father in truth to those who become children of God through faith in Jesus Christ. He is fatherly in His attitude toward all men.[8]

This statement collects the roles of King and Judge and the qualities of great and good under the characteristic of loving

Father. God is pictured as caring for everything in a general way. He is directing history according to his purposes. It indicates the two ways in which God is Father to humankind. The picture of God here is less legal in nature than in the Philadelphia Confession. Further, the freedom-of-God concept is not indicated by this statement.

Since qualities of God discussed in this section were elaborated fully in the first four chapters, it will be more profitable to consider the references of the confessions to God the Son and God the Spirit.

God the Son

In reviewing the early Baptist statements of faith, I was impressed by the fact that most of them contain extensive discussions of the nature and work of Christ. Why? Because the lordship of Christ in the life of the believer and in the church was very real to the early Baptists. It is Christ as revealed in the Scriptures and present in his Spirit who ruled their lives. Further, Christ is recognized as the head of the church.

Whereas the seventeenth-century confessions focused on the offices of Jesus—Prophet, Priest, Mediator, and King—*The Baptist Faith and Message* focuses on those beliefs around which the liberal/fundamentalist controversy raged—divinity of Christ, the virgin birth, Christ's sacrificial death, bodily resurrection, and his triumphant return. This is as one might expect, since confessions are written most often in response to some contemporary crisis.

> Christ is the eternal Son of God. In His incarnation as Jesus Christ he was conceived of the Holy Spirit and born of the virgin Mary. Jesus perfectly revealed and did the will of God, taking upon Himself the demands and necessities of human nature and identifying Himself completely with mankind yet without sin. He honored the divine law by His personal obedience, and in His death on the cross He made provision for the redemption of men from sin. He was raised from the dead with a glorified body and appeared to His disciples as the person who was with them before His crucifixion. He ascended into heaven and is now exalted at the right hand of God where He is the One Mediator, partaking of the nature of God and of man, and in whose Person is effected the

reconciliation between God and man. He will return in power
and glory to judge the world and to consummate His redemptive mission. He now dwells in all believers as the living and ever present Lord.[9]

I will focus on *what* Baptists are affirming about the person and
work of Jesus, and why these beliefs are significant. *The Baptist
Faith and Message* exposition makes seven basic statements
about Jesus.

Christ is the eternal Son of God.—The being of the Son did not
begin at Bethlehem. "In the beginning was the Word . . ."
(John 1:1-14). The Son is eternal.

In the early church the Gnostics attacked the idea that there
was never a time when Christ did not exist. They argued that
he was a spiritual creature issued from the Father.[10] But most
Christians disagreed with this. Today most Christians believe
that the preexistent Christ has always been a part of the Godhead.

Jesus was born of a virgin.—In a miraculous way God's Holy
Spirit caused an egg in the womb of Mary to become fertilized
while she was yet a virgin. In the light of our growing scientific
knowledge of biological process, this belief has been questioned. Yet Stark and Glock found 99 percent of the Southern
Baptists sampled believed in the virgin birth of Jesus.[11]

God is not tame. The free God who created the universe is
surely capable of a miracle of this order. But my concern here
is with *why*. Why should God's Word become incarnate in this
fashion? Here are some suggestions. How better might the
divine-human nature of Jesus Christ be effected? Did it not
dramatize the role of Son and uniqueness of what God was
doing through Jesus? Traditionally, it has been argued that the
virgin birth was necessary for the death of Jesus to have the
power to produce the desired result.[12]

Jesus functioned as a Prophet.—The statement speaks of Jesus
having "perfectly revealed" and done "the will of God." (However, it does so in such a way that the prophetic role of Christ is
hidden in an expression of the belief that Jesus was sinless.)
The fact that Jesus revealed the will of God must not be treated
lightly. The seventeenth-century confessions speak at length of
Jesus' prophetic role.[13] Being the Word of God incarnate, Jesus

had access to the knowledge of God's will. He was on the inside. Jesus is the greatest Prophet. When one wants to know God's will, he must look first to the teachings of our Lord.

I feel that Herschel H. Hobbs's exposition of our statement of faith tends to focus on the redemptive function of Jesus more than on the fact that salvation is for living. Christians should keep a balanced picture of Christianity that emphasizes both its redemptive and its ethical elements.

Jesus is fully human and fully divine.—The Baptist Faith and Message speaks of the manhood of Jesus in terms of his sinlessness and of his obedience to God's will. This was in spite of the fact that he was tempted even as we.

The idea that Jesus was fully human and fully divine is overwhelming. Across the centuries scholarly theologians have argued about how this could be. The tendencies have been either to make the humanity of Jesus only a mask behind which the divine Christ hid, or to make Jesus a particularly good man whom God adopted as his son.

Our tendency to think in terms of substance is the root of the problem. Theologians have tried to state how the stuff of manhood and Godhood could be mixed together in one person (container) without one dominating the other.

The human person that was defined in terms of body, mind, conscience, and will in chapter 5 is also characterized by spirit, or the capacity of self-transcendence. Through the spirit, persons are able, so to speak, to "get outside of themselves" and their life situation and take a critical look. They are not bound by the physical and the social, the here and now of everyday life. It is in and through the spirit that persons are able to communicate with God. Even while emptying himself and accepting the limitations of time and space, Christ's spirit was constantly in communication with God's spirit. Being obedient to God (Phil. 2:7) Jesus' spirit remained in contact with God. Jesus did and taught God's will.

Tempted as we, Jesus did not let the lusts of the flesh dominate him or keep him from doing God's will. He did not allow the power that he exercised to cause him to deny his limitations. He did not allow the enormity of his task to tempt him to half-heartedness or neglect. Although we may not fully understand, we must affirm that "God was in Christ, reconciling the world unto himself" (see 2 Cor. 5:17-21).

Salvation is through Christ.—Our statement of faith affirms that Christ's death "made provision for the redemption of men from sin." This brief statement is as interesting for what it does not say as it is for what it does say. For one thing, it does not deal with the issue debated among early Baptists: Did Christ die for all men or only for the elect? Perhaps this seems unimportant to you; but for our brethren of a few generations ago, it was the test of fellowship. General Baptists affirmed that Christ's death made provision for the salvation of all men, although all might not accept it. Particular Baptists contended that none of Christ's precious blood was to be wasted. He knew before the foundations of the world; in fact, he specifically chose some who would be saved. In recent years, it seems, Baptists have taken a more practical approach as reflected in *The Baptist Faith and Message.*

The exposition of the statement does not get into the debate over how Christ effected our salvation. It does stress the idea that Christ's death was a substitute rather than just an example, but does not argue for Jesus' sacrifice being either a payment to the devil or satisfaction of God's righteousness.[14]

At this point in the early confessions, Baptists discussed Jesus' role as priest. Drawing on the letter to the Hebrews, Baptists saw Jesus both as the sacrificial lamb and as the priest who offered it. In his death the old covenant and the Jewish sacrificial system as a form of worship were finished. Jesus' sacrifice is once for all, and totally sufficient (Heb. 7—10). There is no alternative. Anyone drawing near to God must come through the new covenant which is of grace and made available in the death of Christ.[15]

The resurrection and ascension of Jesus are affirmed.—This affirmation includes several significant points. Baptists believe that Jesus was resurrected from the dead, that his old physical body took on spiritual characteristics, and that he made several post-resurrection appearances to the believers (Luke 24:1-43). Although some in other denominations deny belief in the bodily resurrection of Jesus, most Baptists continue to believe that the free God can perform miracles.[16]

But why did God raise Jesus? Several responses seem valid. It vindicated and glorified Jesus. To perform the role of Suffering Servant was an unparalleled act, and Jesus deserved to be rewarded and to have his name cleared. His appearances solidified the disciples. Whereas they had been quarreling among themselves, after he appeared, they were confirmed in their faith and united in their mission. It made the suffering that they were to endure for him more bearable.

The resurrection gives substance to our hope of eternal life. Jesus is the firstfruits, and we can expect to share in his victory over sin, death, and the law (Rom. 6—7). The ascension dramatized that Jesus is truly the Son of God, that the disciples were being left with a task, and that God would furnish them the power to achieve the task (Luke 24:50-53; Acts 1:9-12).

Jesus is coming again.—The confession affirms belief in Jesus' victorious return to earth. Wisely, the statement is framed in such a way that Baptists of differing persuasions about the events of the return and millennium can maintain fellowship with one another. It is neutral, not affirming or denying any of the basic theories.

Note that Jesus will function in the roles of King and Judge. His work will bring to fulfillment the plan of God for his creation. The redemptive mission will be accomplished. Creation will be perfected.

Christ's Spirit is present with believers.—Baptists affirm that as an earnest of our faith, the Spirit of Christ communicates with the spirits of believers. He is our personal Savior. He is our Lord. The fact that Christ's Spirit indwells believers is amplified by the doctrine of the Holy Spirit.

PERSONAL LEARNING ACTIVITY 20

You have just studied eight basic affirmations *The Baptist Faith and Message* makes about Christ. Without looking back, look at the list below and cross off any statements that are not one of the eight. Then recall one thing you learned from the text about the affirmations that remain on the list. Then look back and check your recall.

1. Christ is the eternal Son of God.
2. Jesus was born of a virgin.
3. Jesus had divine power to work miracles.
4. Jesus functioned as a prophet.
5. Jesus was fully human and fully divine.
6. Salvation is through Christ.

7. **Christ rose from the dead and ascended to the Father.**
8. **Christ indwells the believer.**
9. **Jesus is coming again.**
10. **Believers will spend eternity with Christ after his return.**

God the Holy Spirit

Our current statement of faith has the most satisfactory statement on the Holy Spirit to appear in Baptist confessions. In the early statements, most references to the Spirit discussed the Spirit of Christ. Often these references were brief citations about some part of his work. An attempt at a full statement of the Spirit's nature and work was not found prior to the 1963 statement:

> The Holy Spirit is the Spirit of God. He inspired holy men of old to write the Scriptures. Through illumination He enables men to understand truth. He exalts Christ. He convicts of sin, of righteousness and of judgment. He calls men to the Saviour, and effects regeneration. He cultivates Christian character, comforts believers, and bestows the spiritual gifts by which they serve God through His church. He seals the believer unto the day of final redemption. His presence in the Christian is the assurance of God to bring the believer into the fulness of the stature of Christ. He enlightens and empowers the believer and the church in worship, evangelism, and service.[17]

In interpreting this statement I want to employ three points.

The Spirit is the source of revelation.—The Holy Spirit is the source of and the one who verifies all revelations. When we speak of something being inspired of God, we mean that its source is the Holy Spirit. We also mean that it is authoritative; it demands our attention, respect, and obedience.

Unfortunately, the church has been confronted by false teachers who have claimed the authority of the Spirit to gain acceptance for their own teachings. How are we to distinguish between that which is inspired by God's Spirit and that which is not? Baptists have contended that the basic revelation of God and his will is to be found in the life and teachings of Jesus

Christ. Each new idea that is advanced should be tested as to its compliance with the spirit of the teachings of Jesus.

The popularity of the charismatic movement in recent years makes this a practical admonition. The following questions must be asked of the charismatics: Is the movement so individualistic that it neglects the social (or communal) functions of the church? Is it out of balance, focusing on only a part of the gospel? How is Christ's command to love practiced in relationships with noncharismatics? What safeguards are taken to test the spirits?

The Spirit is mediator of God's saving grace.—The Holy Spirit works with the lost. This work can be divided into three stages. Initially, the Spirit convicts of sin, righteousness, and judgment (John 16:7-16). This is what might be called the negative function of the Spirit. Most of us go through life satisfied with ourselves. To change we must first become dissatisfied. This is what the Spirit does. He makes us realize that we are sinning by living contrary to the expressed commands of God. He makes us see that a different kind of life is what God wants. And he teaches us that we will be held responsible for our failure to do God's will. (This function is one the Spirit continues to perform even after our conversion.)

The Spirit "calls men (humankind) to the Savior." Once he has made us dissatisfied with the way we are and the way we do, he points us to the one who has the solution we seek. The framers of the confession acted wisely by passing issues among early Baptists. Does the Spirit call all men or only those predestined to salvation? And do those who are called have the freedom to reject God's call, or must they accept it? Most Southern Baptists today are far too practical to worry about these questions, but they were tests of fellowship for our forefathers.[18]

The other service provided for sinners by the Spirit is that of regeneration. This means the new birth. The thrust of the New Testament teaching about salvation is that converts become new people. Attitudes, priorities, values, life-style, and world view are either changed or radically rearranged. The convert feels cleansed. He experiences the joy of forgiveness. His spirit and the Spirit of God engage in communication with each other.

The Spirit is present with believers.—This leads us to the third general area of the Spirit's work—his activity with believers. The statement lists several things that the Spirit does for us.

For one thing, he continues work on our personalities. The Christian life should be one of growth toward spiritual maturity. The Holy Spirit makes this possible by showing us our shortcomings, by showing us our strengths, and by empowering us to overcome the one and use the other more effectively. In the language of Paul, the Spirit helps us prune away the fruits of the flesh, replacing them with the fruits of the Spirit—fruits that the Spirit cultivates (Gal. 5:7-25).

What about gifts of the Spirit (1 Cor. 12—14)? "The Baptist Faith and Message" statement stresses the important point that the purpose of gifts is for the service of God through the church. Those who have gifts have special responsibility. Gifts may become the occasion for sins of pride. Those who are endowed with gifts should use them for the building up of the church to the glory of God. We should be thankful to God for having provided some with unique gifts because they have appeared in crises to serve his church, carrying it on to victory. Think about the work of the apostles; think about the history of our denomination. Let us pray that we never become so worldly, so highly structured that we cannot recognize the gifts God has given to men and women to build us up.[19]

The relationship of the Spirit to the believer, as all personal relationships, has both instrumental and expressive qualities. In times of trouble the knowledge that God loves us and has evidenced his love by the indwelling of his Spirit comforts us. His presence assures us that we will be made perfect, that we will be like Christ. Further, the indwelling Spirit enlightens and empowers. This knowledge and this skill is to be used for the accomplishment of the essential tasks of the church—worship, evangelism, and service.

CONCLUSION

Baptists believe in one God. However, we share with the writers of the New Testament the belief that God is known as Father, Son, and Spirit, that these are three persons with one essence. Limited as we are in our understanding by the categories of space and time, we cannot explain fully how this can be. But we realize that God as spirit is not limited. He does many things that transcend our power to comprehend. We affirm the doctrine of the Trinity because it fits our experience with God.

I noted that in the language of sociology, people become people through interaction with other people. We are a part of everyone we have ever met. If we can accept the idea that for God to be person he needed to interact with other persons, then we can say that he must have been eternally Triune. For him to be perfect person, the interaction should have been with other perfect persons.[20] If this argument is correct, then the doctrine of the Trinity must be accepted by those who believe in God.

In this chapter I have outlined what Baptist statements or confessions of faith have had to say about the nature and work of the three persons of the Trinity. I indicated wherein "The Baptist Faith and Message" was an improvement over earlier confessions and where it omitted concepts that I think are important. In all likelihood some readers will not agree with my evaluation. Not being a creedal people, Baptists have always been willing in quest of truth to discuss differences in a spirit of love and openness.

PERSONAL LEARNING ACTIVITY 21
In what ways is a statement or confession of faith different from a creed? What is the function of a statement or confession of faith for Baptists? Do you see any tendency for our statements or confessions to take on the function of creeds?

NOTES

1. One of the best sources for a discussion of these doctrinal disputes is Reinhold Seeberg, *Textbook of the History of Doctrines* (Grand Rapids: Baker Book House, 1952). For discussion of these disputes set in the historical situation, you might consult Williston Walker, *A History of the Christian Church* (New York: Charles Scribner's Sons, 1959) or Robert A. Baker, *A Summary of Christian History* (Nashville: Broadman Press, 1959). Baker is church historian at Southwestern Baptist Theological Seminary.

2. Emil Brunner, *The Christian Doctrine of God, Dogmatics: Vol. I* (Philadelphia: The Westminster Press, 1950), p. 210.

3. Henry Pitney Van Dusen, *Spirit, Son and Father* (New York: Charles Scribner's Sons, 1958).

4. This statement is available in tract form. But my reference, with the exception of quoted selections from the statement, will be to

a reprint in Dr. Hobbs's exposition of the statement or confession, Herschel H. Hobbs, *The Baptist Faith and Message* (Nashville: Convention Press, 1971).

Also, I want to reiterate the distinction between confession and creed. A creed is something that a believer is supposed to affirm. It is a test of faith. If someone is not willing to affirm it, he is excluded from the fellowship. A confession is much less binding. It has no authority in itself. It is not lent authority by the church. It is simply a guideline, a bench mark. It is to assist, not to dominate the believer.

5. From "The Baptist Faith and Message" statement.

6. William L. Lumpkin, *Baptist Confessions of Faith* (Philadelphia: The Judson Press, 1959), p. 393. Lumpkin has rendered a great service by collecting many of the confessions of faith and interpreting them in terms of their historical setting.

7. *Ibid.*, p. 362.

8. From "The Baptist Faith and Message" statement.

9. *Ibid.*

10. See Seeberg, *op. cit.*, or Walker, *op. cit.*

11. Rodney Stark and Charles Y. Glock, *American Piety* (Berkeley and Los Angeles: University of California Press, 1968), p. 34.

12. Walter Thomas Conner, *Revelation and God* (Nashville: Broadman Press, 1936), pp. 157-60.

13. Lumpkin, *op. cit.*, pp. 158-60.

14. Gustaf Aulén, *Christus Victor* (New York: The Macmillan Co., 1961). This is a good introduction to the various theories of the atonement.

15. See "Hebrews," *The Broadman Bible Commentary*, Vol. 12 (Nashville: Broadman Press, 1972).

16. Stark and Glock, *op. cit.*, p. 36.

17. Hobbs, *op. cit.*, p. 33.

18. William L. Lumpkin, *Baptist Foundations in the South* (Nashville: Broadman Press, 1961).

19. Hugh Wamble, *Through Trial to Triumph* (Nashville: Convention Press, 1958).

20. This concept was developed by American philosopher-social psychologist George Herbert Mead. See *On Social Psychology*, ed. by Anselm Strauss (Chicago: University of Chicago Press, 1964).

Chapter 7

"We Want to Thank You, Lord, . . ."

Gist's Creek Baptist Church sits almost hidden in the slate knobs of Sevier County, Tennessee. Only fifteen miles from the Gatlinburg resort area, it is light years away culturally. I was rather new to the Appalachian area when I was asked to supply preach there. Their gospel songs, their altar calls when everyone came forward and prayed simultaneously, and their mountain manners took some getting used to. And I imagine that they found the flatlands college professor a bit peculiar. We grew to love one another, and I came to appreciate their faith in God. We worshiped the same Lord, howbeit in somewhat different ways. It was at Gist's Creek that I first heard this prayer line: "We thank you, Lord, for letting us live one more week so we could come out to your house this Sunday morning to worship you with all our friends." I noticed that whoever prayed in the opening exercises prayed this sentence.

Since then, I have noted that this same sentence is prayed in many other churches. Initially, I labeled it an expression of the well-known mountaineer fatalism. Perhaps it is. But it is more. It reflects a time in our heritage when life was hard. People lived a day at a time. To have made it through another week in a hostile land was an accomplishment. It was truly something to thank God for.

The first church in this section of the country was named Providence. Perhaps this was significant. Fatalism takes away strength. It cuts the nerve. It allows us to become calloused. Fatalists are too complacent, too accepting of the success of evil in this world. But this is not the problem of most of us. We have restricted God's activity. We are confident of our own abilities to run our lives and the world as well. God has been removed from the throne and demoted to a position on the emergency squad. Somewhere between the optimism of some and the fatalism of others there is a place for a well-thought-out doctrine of God's providence.

MEANING OF PROVIDENCE

The basic idea of the doctrine of providence is that God is active in history. On the one hand, he is keeping things from falling apart. On the other, he is moving things toward his appointed ends. God has not turned things loose.[1]

Normally, theologians distinguish between God's *general* and his *special* providence. Special providence means that God is concerned with special things, events, and individuals and works his will through them and in them. General providence means that in various ways he blesses all humankind.

To find a full statement of what Baptists have believed about the doctrine of providence (and the related doctrines of election and predestination) one has to go back to the mid-seventeenth century and the Second London Confession:

> God, the good Creator of all things, in his infinite power, and wisdom, doth uphold, direct, dispose, and govern all Creatures, and all things, from the greatest even to the least, by his most wise and holy providence, to the end for the which they were Created; according unto his infallible fore-knowledge, and the free and immutable Councel of his own will; to the praise of the glory of his wisdom, power, justice, infinite goodness and mercy.

General Providence

In this first paragraph early Baptists affirmed God's general providence. They declared that God is active in his creation at the broadest, most basic level possible. He is the one standing behind the laws of nature that keep things moving along in a stable, orderly fashion (Matt. 5:45; 6:25-34; 10:29-31). Modern science has learned much about the laws governing the processes of the mineral, plant, and animal kingdoms. Ours is an orderly world. Ecologists tell us that creation is an unbelievable, well-balanced system with the various parts dependent on one another.

Here is the truth of the basic ethical principle of the ancient Stoics. They taught that wise persons learn what the laws of nature are and live accordingly. For example, those who eat excessively can anticipate heart disease; those who smoke heavily, lung problems; those who use alcohol excessively, liver disorders. Mankind has learned that when societies fail to practice conservation and sanitation, deep distresses and miseries follow.

The basic point is that God's general providence is a frame for our activities. On one hand, it provides an orderly, dependable place for us to live out our lives. But in doing this it sets limits on our freedom. And when we break these limits, knowingly or in ignorance, we likely will suffer the consequences.

The confession adds, however, that God has not bound himself by these laws. Miracles can and do happen. When they do, they are noteworthy because they are scarce and unique.

A related doctrine of the church is that of common grace. God has given humankind a sense of oughtness. He has given us basic insights into right and wrong. Thereby humankind is kept from becoming as evil as it might otherwise become (Rom. 1).

Consequently, one reason that the good people of the Gist's Creek flock are able to worship God on any given Sunday is the result of God's general providence and common grace. God has provided us with an orderly world in which to live out our lives.

PERSONAL LEARNING ACTIVITY 22
Before studying further take time to think and write out your own definition of God's providence. After you have studied this chapter, come back to the definition and rework it to include any new ideas you have learned.

Special Providence
The second paragraph of the confession attends to the belief that although God is the ultimate cause of everything that happens, at the secondary level, where we mortals live out our lives, there is at least the appearance of freedom:

> Although in relation to the foreknowledge and Decree of God, the first cause, all things come to pass immutably and infallibly; so that there is not any thing, befalls any by chance, or without his Providence; yet by the same Providence he

> ordered them to fall out, according to the nature of second causes, either necessarily, freely, or contingently.

This statement reflects the effort of the seventeenth-century theologians to deal with the issue of causation and responsibility, of determinism and freewill.[2]

The older theologians were suggesting that God is the ultimate cause of all that happens in two ways: first, in the sense that he knew from before the moment he created existence what the outcome would be. The whole panorama of world history, down to the most trivial event, was known to him. Therefore, God might have concluded by some calculus of cost-benefit that the whole project was not worth the trouble and not have created the universe. Or conceivably, he might have created it in some other way. Yet he set the project in motion even though he knew the consequences. This act is the other way in which God is the ultimate cause of all that happens: he is the Creator of the world in which things occur. This statement affirms the ultimate sovereignty of God. That which befalls us is caused by God at least in this rather indirect sense and must therefore have some purpose.

However, this level of causation is far distant from our everyday world. At the level where events happen within history—where the things God foreknew actually occur—a different order of causation applies. Three categories are listed by the framers of the confession—necessary, free, and contingent.

Necessary cause.—By *necessary cause* the framers of the confession meant that some events occur and there does not appear to be anything anyone could have done to have stopped them. An example of this might be the so-called "acts of God" that are mentioned in insurance policies. No person can be held responsible for the occurrence of a tornado, an earthquake, or a flood. Generally, this category includes the normal working out of God's general providence in history.

Free cause.—By *free* cause the framers of the confession meant those events that are the result of the choice of a specific person or group of persons. Knowing what we know today about all the social forces that affect our choices, there are few things we do that are really by free choice. Yet the practice of developing and pursuing projects, as discussed in chapter 5, is grounded in the capacity of people to make choices. From a vast variety of possible alternatives I make choices about what the long- and short-range goals for my life will be. I select from a variety of possible means of achieving these goals. I set priorities and order my life in terms of my goals. In all of this I am relatively free; consequently, I am responsible.[3]

Contingent cause.—Standing between the necessary and the free is the *contingent*. For example, when I took employment as a professor at Carson-Newman College, I placed myself under the authority of the administration of the college. I became responsible for preparing to teach my classes, for evaluating their performance, and for working harmoniously with my colleagues. This choice will have significant effects on our family. Consider our children. Who their friends are, who they marry, the kind of educational and cultural experiences they have, and their world view will be affected by this choice. The point is that a relatively free choice may have a variety of unanticipated results that grow out of that choice.

Here responsibility is more difficult to fix. Many of the things I do with my time, energy, and money are a result of and depend on my employment as a teacher. They take on the qualities of necessity. However, if I find that some of the demands within the role of teacher are causing me to do things that I feel are wrong, or if I feel that the costs are greater than the benefits, I must reconsider my choice. Specifically, I ought to consider trying to change the system that causes me to do these things, move to another school, change professions, or perhaps change some of the things that make it difficult for me to do my job.

Summary

What the early Baptists were confessing, then, was a belief in a truly sovereign God, one not limited by our actions. In a passive sense God knows everything from the great events of the natural universe to the significant turns of history; to the lesser events of everyday life of persons, groups, organizations, and institutions; to our own thoughts even before we think them. Even though he knew all of this, God created things as he did. And since God is known as great and good, this must be the best possible world for achieving God's goals with the means available.

Further, the early Baptists were confessing their beliefs, that God, in the active sense, was moving history toward his appointed ends. Everything that happens in the lives of individuals; to families; to clubs, churches, businesses, and all kinds of organizations and institutions; to nations; and to creation itself is caused by God. Looking at life from this perspective, it is comforting to know that whatever befalls us has some purpose in the mind of God. This can help us find meaning in the face of suffering. However, when pushed to its logical conclusion, this doctrine is filled with problems. Although it is helpful to see God behind what happens to us (and all events having some meaning, directly or indirectly), it can result in a self-defeating kind of fatalism. For example, a rather typical response to this kind of an affirmation might be: "Okay, if God is the cause of everything that happens, 'what is to be, will be'; so why should I bother myself with anything? I can accept the evil of society. I will not get upset about sin. I will not even witness my faith to the lost. I'll just sit here and take what comes."

Of course, this kind of attitude is not biblical. The disciples and members of the early church were actively evangelical. The prophets spoke out against the personal and social evils of their age as did Jesus in his. There is no fatalism or complacency in the Bible; rather there is urgency.

Here is the basic paradox that divided the early Baptists. Some stressed the idea of God's being the cause of everything and drifted toward fatalism. Others emphasized the freedom and responsibility of humankind and drifted toward the concept that God's knowledge is limited. But most lived with the paradox. God is the ultimate cause of all things, at least in the passive sense of knowing what will happen. Yet at the secondary level there are choices for us to make, choices of free and of contingent causation. We are responsible for these choices. God is God. As sovereign, free God he has chosen to hold us responsible for our acts. The fact that he knew beforehand what our choice would be, that he conditioned our choices by general and active special providence, and that his ultimate will will be accomplished regardless of our acts does not free us of responsibility. And since he is God it is his place, not ours, to decide what our responsibility is.

PERSONAL LEARNING ACTIVITY 23
Check your understanding of ultimate cause and contingent causation. Then read Acts 16:36-40; Numbers 14:1-24; and Acts 5:32-37 and answer the following questions about each event.
1. What was God's ultimate purpose at that time—that is, toward what end was God moving in the way he was leading the persons in the passage?
2. What was the contingent causation—that is, in exercising their freedom to choose, did the persons in the passage follow God's leading and what was the result of their decision?
3. If the persons did not choose to follow God's leadership, was his ultimate cause accomplished anyhow? How?

It may not be consistent in terms of formal logic to affirm that God is the ultimate cause of all things, and yet declare that people are responsible for their actions. But this is what the Scriptures teach, and this is what life confirms.

SOME ISSUES

This same confession that informed most of our Baptist forefathers in seventeenth-century England and in Colonial America, continued by discussing four topics that might have been a problem for some.

Miracles and Special Providence

The first was God's active special providence, including miracles.

> God in his ordinary Providence maketh use of means; yet is free to work, without, above, and against them at his pleasure.[4]

Quite simply this paragraph affirms that God's standard operating procedure is to support and work within the laws of nature which have their source in him. But this does not mean that he has bound himself by these laws. In the pursuit of his goals, God is free to suspend or to transcend these laws. The miracles of the virgin birth, the resurrection, and the ascension of Jesus are key examples of this freedom. Because of God's general providence, the miraculous is truly out of the ordinary. Yet it is always a possibility.

Further, I take this statement to be an affirmation of God's active special providence. God acts on the plane of history empowering, punishing, inspiring, rewarding, and comforting individuals, groups, and nations as he seeks to accomplish his purpose. God is not just the producer of the dramas of history. He is also the director and an actor.

God and Sin
Second, it is argued that although God created the world in such a way that sin was possible, knew that it would occur, and even included its reality in the development of his plan for creation, he is not to be blamed for its appearance. We probably have heard this point discussed. "Why did a good God create a world in which sin might occur? Why did he allow it, if he is all powerful?" Perhaps it was to give man a real choice.

Who are we to judge God—puny creatures whose knowledge is limited by time and space? God has demonstrated in his dealing with humankind that he is great, good, loving, and free. I am forced to conclude that he created the kind of world that fitted his purposes.

Certainly the effects of sin are terrible in the lives of individuals, institutions, nations, and all of creation. But had it not been for sin in the world, would we have known God's love as well as we do? Would we have been as thankful to God for his graciousness? Would we have been as aware of our dependence upon him? It has been true always, "It is the bitter that makes the sweet." As bad as sin is, if God's purpose was to bind man to him in the community of love, it is impossible to imagine a better way.

God and Suffering
The third issue dealt with in the confession is the fact that it is sometimes the lot of the saved to suffer. This reminds us that in its popular usage providence often refers to the blessings God provides for us. Frequently, we speak of his providential

care. So many good things happen to us that can be explained in no other way.

As I look back across my life, I see God's providential hand leading, guiding, directing me. Sometimes I was aware of what he was doing. Other times I became aware only after the fact. Committed Christians are predisposed to seeing God's working in their lives. And when we reflect on our experiences, we realize this. Bits and pieces that made little sense at the time later fall into place, and we suddenly realize what God was doing. God uses it all to help us mature as well as to serve his kingdom (Heb. 12:1-17).

I feel sorry for those who do not have this sense of being important to God. It must be difficult for a person who does not feel important to God to find meaning in this world.

Back in BSU days I worried about finding the right girl to marry. I prayed and sought God's will. I see now that God was preparing Jackie and me for each other. I was concerned about what kind of work to do. And now I can see that God has prepared me to do some special kinds of things for him. Now I am confronted with other problems. But based on my past experiences, I am confident that as I stay close to the Lord and face these problems, he will continue to help me mature and will achieve through me some modest goals for his kingdom. Many of you who are reading this book can offer similar testimony.

What about those times and places and lives where the providential care of God is not visible at crucial moments? Although she is one of the sweetest, most gentle Christians I have ever known, one of the women of our town is slowly, painfully dying of cancer. Although he was a brilliant Christian scholar and a model to all of us for his integrity, a friend was struck and killed by an automobile loaded with drunks. The son of what I thought was the perfect family failed in an attempted suicide and is left with the mind of an eight-year-old. Although he had recently retired and was able really to help our church, our treasurer suffered a heart attack and died. Although he was active in the church, my friend's business failed. Although he sought to bring peace in a racially troubled community, a political acquaintance was not returned to Congress by his constituency. Defeat, pain, financial ruin, suffering, death—are experienced by the good people as well as by the bad. It seems that sometimes God's providential care breaks down. Why? How can we fit these events into the concept that God is the cause of everything that befalls us and still confess that God is good?

You, too, know of similar cases. And when we are honest, such instances trouble us more and offer a greater trial to our faith than all the new theologies and sects that appear. "Why, God, did you let this terrible thing happen to me, my family, my friend, my church, my company, my nation?" We are troubled by these events that seem not to mesh with our belief that God is great, good, and loving.

Frankly, I have not been able, to my own satisfaction, to find meaning in all of these cases I have cited. I am afraid of the simple answers like those in some memorial obituaries for young children. A recent one declared that God "called home" little Johnny because heaven needed his childish smile. I cannot accept the fatalistic assessment "his number was up" to explain what I know was the error of a physician. Nor am I comfortable with the proposal that there must be suffering in this world, so God sends it upon the good because they are better able to handle it. I would, however, like to suggest some factors that should be taken into consideration when we attempt an understanding of the suffering of the good. Suffering comes from a variety of sources and causes and has a variety of consequences. In what follows I will attempt to categorize some of these.

Breaking the laws of nature.—Some of the suffering that befalls the good is a consequence of their breaking of the laws of nature, willfully or in ignorance. I have a friend who is angry with God for letting his wife lie in a coma for seven years before her death. She was a good woman who loved her family and her church. However, she also loved sweets. And she was a diabetic. She would not follow her diet. The coma was the consequence of not caring for herself properly. I do not know why God allowed her to linger so long in a comatose state, but I am aware of some valuable consequences for the church and the community as the people cared for her during those years. God has not promised to place a protective bubble around Christians so that we can do anything we please. If we break the laws of nature, we, like anyone else, are responsible for the consequences.

The complexities of social life.—Life is lived in relationships with other persons. All of our actions have either direct or indirect effects on others. When I make choices, no matter how noble my motives, I may be causing others to suffer. Likewise, the choices others make affect me. Our choices of consumer goods help some producers and hurt others.

But consider the consequences when our choices are made with selfish, vindictive, spiteful motives in mind. Or again, consider when we are lazy and careless. Through exercising choice in these ways, we bring much suffering on ourselves and on others as well. For example, a lazy, irresponsible physician can cause great suffering for others. A vindictive politician can cause hundreds of people to lose their livelihood.

Not only are we bound up in relationship with one another, we are participants in a variety of social institutions—families, clubs, churches, and other groups. We are parts of businesses, governments, and other massive organizations. We are citizens of nations. We dwell in the ongoing stream of history. If, even with the best of motives, we cannot interact directly with one another without causing some hurt, how can we expect to operate within this vast web of society without some hurt resulting?[5]

Looking at society as I do from the perspective of a sociologist, I am convinced that there will be evil and suffering and injustice as long as people and institutions are selfish and as long as resources are limited. As Christians standing in the heritage of the biblical prophets, we must struggle against the evil. But although we may win some battles, and we may lose more frequently, the final victory awaits the end of time and the coming of Jesus as King.

But why does God wait? Why does he not come now and set things right? Sincere believers have posed this question for generations. With the problems of the spread of communism, the rising power of atheism and secularism, the threat of overpopulation, the crisis of pollution, and the specter of worldwide starvation, it seems that now would be an opportune day for Jesus to come again. But so were the black days of the world wars, the bubonic plague, the Muslim conquest of the Near East, the sacking of Rome by the Huns. The fact that there is so much personal and social evil in the world makes it necessary that the good God come in judgment and set things right. But he will come by his own timetable, not ours.

The power of the demon.—Satan is not yet bound (Rev. 20). The forces of evil are real. In their freedom people often choose to do the will of the devil. He is powerful. He will continue to hurt the good, hoping to turn them against God (Job). He will continue to tempt people to evil in their interpersonal relations and through the institutions they control (Rev. 1—3). And God will sometimes punish and make those who have rejected him suffer (Hab. 1). Actually we live in a war zone. Consequently, for a variety of reasons we will see suffering, much of it appearing unfair to us.

Growth toward maturity.—Suffering may be redemptive. Job seems to have been better for it (Job 38—41). So were Peter (John 21) and Paul (2 Cor. 11—12). Some of the finest Christians I know are people who have been tempered by the fires of suffering. "The purest gold is refined in the hottest fire." Although God may not cause suffering in order to produce growth toward maturity, he can see that growth toward maturity results from suffering when it does come.

> We know that in everything God works for good with those who love him, who are called according to his purpose. For those whom he foreknew he also predestined to be conformed to the image of his Son, in order that he might be the first-born among many brethren. And those whom he predestined he also called; and those whom he called he also justified; and those whom he justified he also glorified (Rom. 8:28-30, RSV).

This passage is affirming what the Second London Confession states. God knows, and he is working through what happens to us to help us toward maturity. Therefore, if we are among the elect, we will respond to the occasions of suffering, as well as to the occasions of blessing, to grow toward being in the likeness of the Son. In a real sense this is the proof of our salvation.

Confusion about God.—Many things trouble us because of our wrong understanding of the nature, purpose, and will of God. I still remember one August night when I was twelve years old. The Kansas City Blues baseball team was leading the old American Association. My dad and I were listening to a crucial game with the Toledo Mudhens. In the bottom of the ninth inning, the Mudhens staged a rally. I prayed that the Blues would turn them back. They didn't; we lost. I burst into tears. When Dad asked why I was crying, I told him that God had not done what I had asked him to do. I could not understand why God was so cruel. "Maybe there is no God," I sobbed. Wisely, Dad replied, "Do you suppose that some young boys in Toledo were praying for the Mudhens?"

What a spot to put God in. However the game ended, someone would be angry with God. Yet we put God in this "hotbox" frequently. For him to give me certain pleasure, he would be required to cause someone else to be sad. God is not "the great vending machine in the sky." He is not in the business of serving me, or you. He operates in a completely different way. When we attempt to reduce God to our servant, we are bound to be disappointed.

These five points that I have sketched briefly do not answer all of the specific problems that I cited earlier in this section. But they can provide a way to look at the problems. One of the most important functions of religion is to help believers find meaning for what happens so they can understand life as it is experienced. The old confession declares:

> So that whatsoever befalls any of his elect is by his appointment, for his glory, and their good.[6]

Problems come because of a variety of reasons: our sin, the sin of others, the natural order, the character of the societal environment, satanic temptation, God's punishment, and even our own misunderstanding of what is happening. God has created a world that is complex. He works in society at many levels. In accomplishing a goal at one level, suffering may occur at another (that is, to keep his promise to the Hebrew nation, individual Canaanites had to suffer). For Christians, the end result of suffering can be their good and God's glory. This is true regardless of the immediate source of the suffering.

PERSONAL LEARNING ACTIVITY 24
You have just studied five sources or causes of suffering in the life of a Christian. List these down the left side of a sheet of paper. Then write beside each some hardship or suffering that has resulted from that source or cause.

Election and God

The fourth problem area dealt with in the old confession is the explanation of the fact that some people are not converted. If one believes that God is the ultimate cause of everything, it would seem logically to follow that he not only elects some to salvation, he also predestines some to damnation. The Second London Confession attempted to soften this by contending that God was justified in doing this because of their sins which he foreknew. It suggests that he gives up on some and turns them over to Satan. Some early Baptists did not accept this Calvinistic position. Under the influence of the Continental Anabaptists, they emphasized the responsibility of humankind before God. To be responsible one must be free either to accept or to reject God. Some moved to a position that God is finite, not knowing beforehand what the choice of a man will be. Others simply stated that whereas God knows beforehand what choice a particular person will make, within the frame of history God's call is addressed to everyone, and each person is free to accept or to reject it. At the secondary level freedom of causation is affirmed, and with it responsibility.

Under the impact of the Great Awakening revivals of the eighteenth century, most Baptists in America accepted this modified Calvinist position. They rejected "double-barreled" predestination, on the one hand, and the image of God being finite on the other. As "The Baptist Faith and Message" puts it, God's election is "consistent with the free agency of man."[7] God calls. He knows when he does who will respond. And we are responsible for our answer to God. This seems to fit both the biblical witness and our experience.

By "free agency" Baptists do not mean that God is some kind of peddler who shows us his wares, and then we rationally decide whether to buy from him. Rather, God comes as the Judge, King, and Father. He comes demanding our obedience. If, as we may, we reject him, we will suffer the consequences.

CONCLUSION

When the good people at Gist's Creek prayed, thanking God for letting them live one more week so they could come to worship him with their friends, they were expressing a basic element in our Baptist doctrine of God. Truly, God is a providential God. He created an orderly universe so that they might know what to expect from nature and order their lives accordingly. Truly God has moved in history so that they would be free to worship him according to the dictates of their hearts. Truly, he has called them to salvation so that they would want to worship him. Truly God has blessed them each in many special ways.

Of course, the saints of Gist's Creek have experienced evil and have had their measure of suffering. It has come for all of the reasons mentioned earlier. But their life experience has been such that they know that God is good. They know that the evil and suffering that has befallen them has meaning at some level—personal growth toward maturity, witness to others, or his goals for institutions, the nation, or all of creation. Directly or indirectly whatever happens serves God's purposes. And claiming Paul's promise (Rom. 8:28), they have matured. Like all of us they question; they do not always understand. But they keep the faith. They believe that God is dependable. He will keep his promises. He will win the victory. They believe that at the end of time God will balance the books and make everything right.

Yet, can the people on Gist's Creek pray anything else? If God is the ultimate cause of everything, if he knows every event in history before it occurs, can they pray asking him for anything, really? When they ask for a friend to be cured of a sickness, for someone to be saved, or for the end of a conflict, can their prayers be effective?

Jesus taught believers to ask God for things they needed (Matt. 7:7-12). Is this only a kind of therapy for us, or can God's will be influenced by our prayers? Does the fact that God has foreknowledge of everything and in this sense is the ultimate cause of everything, mean that there is no flexibility in God's plan? Does prayer really change things, or only us? Apparently Jesus hoped that the Father might change his plan when he prayed in the garden (Luke 22:39-46).

Certainly, God expects the elect to live in communion with him. Prayer is an integral part of this communion. Communion always affects the persons involved. As a person God is affected by our prayers. Like any good father, he is pleased when his children come to him. Even though God may know that I am going to pray to him about something, and even though he knows beforehand that he will modify things because I asked him, will this make the event any less significant to him or to me when it happens? The saints on Gist's Creek can pray to God in the assurance that he will be listening and will be affected by their prayers.

As you see, the doctrine of God's providence is complicated. It is hoped that this study has furnished some light. Questions remain, but we believe that God is great, good, loving, and free. In his own time and in his own way, he will work things out. Some of us may suffer unjustly in this life. But there is a life to come. There God will reign supreme. We rest in this hope.

PERSONAL LEARNING ACTIVITY 25
Go back to Personal Learning Activity 22 and re-work your definition of God's providence.

NOTES

1. L. Berkhof, *Systematic Theology* (4th rev. and enl. ed.; Grand Rapids: William B. Eerdmans Publishing Co., 1949), pp. 100-25, 165-78.

2. A. C. Underwood, *A History of English Baptists* (London: The Carey Kingsgate Press Limited, 1947, 1956).

3. Gibson Winter, *The Elements for a Social Ethic* (New York: The Macmillan Co., 1966). Winter does an excellent job of developing a theory of social action. He demonstrates that everyday life is intentional.

4. William L. Lumpkin, *Baptist Confessions of Faith* (Philadelphia: The Judson Press, 1959), pp. 256-57.

5. Peter Blau, *Power and Social Exchange*. This is a significant book in that it develops the complexities of the social web in which we live and act.

6. Lumpkin, *op.cit.*, p. 257.

7. From "The Baptist Faith and Message" statement.

Chapter 8

"The Shadow of a Mighty Rock"

*Because our understanding of God is so incomplete, he uses a
number of different means to make our understanding of him
more complete. He uses messengers, he appears in nature, and
he is known by way of simile or analogy to things in everyday
experience. One of the most frequently used analogies is rock.*

Like many town boys who have had the opportunity, I looked
forward to the times when we would go to visit Grandmother
on her farm. She lived in what seemed to me to be an immense
old white house just outside Greenridge, Missouri. Her kitchen
provided all those things that please young boys. Her yard was
dominated by several large pear trees that provided both challenge and opportunity for boys to prove their strength and
daring. Feeding chickens, hunting eggs, milking the cow,
watching the threshers—these were high moments for this
town boy.

I suppose the most unusual thing about Grandmother Farley
was that she liked to fish. Sometimes she would take my cousins
and me down to the spring-fed creek that meandered across
the back of her farm. She would bait our hooks; and while we
waited for some activity, she would tell us about when our
parents were young. One story that pleased us all was that my
cousins' mother and my father had been baptized in the very
pool where we were fishing. She told of how the people came
from town and sang and had a wonderful time that day.

Some days the fish would not cooperate, and we would grow
restless. Then Grandmother would pick up flat creek rocks and
show us how to make them skip across the pool. Fishing poles
laid aside, we would search the gravel bar for the best rocks.
Then a friendly competition would develop to see who could
get the most skips out of a rock. Sometimes one of us would
find a piece of flint some ancient craftsman had made into an

arrow or a spear point. And that night we would dream of the long ago when Indian boys about our size probably had skipped flat rocks across our pool.

When God called Abraham and made a covenant with him, the Stone Age still flourished. Centuries later after the Exodus and the Conquest, the Philistines were able to exercise dominance over the Hebrews because they held a monopoly on the skill of iron working. Only with the Davidic kingdom did the Jews move into the Iron Age.

For most of us, stones are something to which we pay little attention unless they are the sparkling gem kind. But Stone-Age man was different. He used stones for obtaining and preparing food, for protection, for shelter, and even for worship. His survival depended on his skill with rocks. He was trained from childhood to fashion tools from stones. He could see how a rough stone could be made into something useful. He knew which of the different kinds of stones were best for the particular tool he needed to make. And from that type he could pick one that had the right shape, grain, and/or feel.

Stone-Age man knew that what distinguished him from the animals he hunted was his ability to use rocks. So he attached an importance to rocks that some might suggest is carried over into the present-day activities of rock hounds, the giving of diamond rings, the "pet rock" craze, and the symbol for a successful insurance company.

MEANING OF "GOD IS A ROCK"

It was not idle chatter when Moses, David, Isaiah, Jeremiah, and others called God a rock. It was a great compliment. It was God, the rock of Israel, who provided stability to the universe, security for his people, salvation, strength, and victory. Rock and the related terms, stone and mountain, were particularly effective symbols for speaking of God. They gather up much of what the Bible declares about God; therefore, I will use these symbols to summarize the teachings of *The Doctrine of God*.

Consider some of the occasions when God's presence and revelation of self was related to a rock, stone, or mountain. At Bethel Jacob lay down on the ground to sleep, taking a stone for a pillow. After his vision in which he received a blessing from God, Jacob used that stone to mark the place where he

had met God (Gen. 28:10-22). Moses brought from the mountain the laws of God, written on stone tablets (Ex. 19—28). One
means of exacting the death penalty from those who broke
these laws of God was to stone them (Deut. 22:21-24). When
the Hebrews needed water, God instructed Moses to strike a
rock. When the Hebrews finally crossed the Jordan into the
Promised Land, they erected a memorial of twelve stones so
that following generations could know what God had done
(Josh. 4:19-24). Gideon tore down the standing stones at the
pagan high place. He and many others built altars of stone
(Judg. 6:24-27). David used stones to kill Goliath (1 Sam.
17:41-54). When Solomon built the Temple, he did so on
Mount Moriah (Zion), God's holy mountain. Sacrifices were
made on a large rock there. The Temple itself was constructed
of expertly fashioned stones (1 Kings 5:17 to 6:13). God's glory
dwelt in this house made of stone (1 Kings 8:9-15).

On numerous occasions the psalmist and the prophets refer
to God as the rock. Typical of the emphasis of these is this
statement:

> Blessed be the Lord, my rock, who trains my hands for war,
> and my fingers for battle; my rock and my fortress, my
> stronghold and my deliverer, my shield and he in whom I
> take refuge, who subdues the peoples under him (Ps. 144:1-2,
> RSV).

In what is probably a messianic passage, Isaiah declares:

> Behold, a king will reign in righteousness, and princes will
> rule in justice. Each will be like a hiding place from the wind,
> a covert from the tempest, like streams of water in a dry
> place, like the shade of a great rock in a weary land (Isa.
> 32:1-2, RSV).

Our God is a rock—dependable, protective, victorious.

It is interesting that when Jesus, the Son of God, affirmed his
divinity in response to Peter's confession at Caesarea Philippi,
he said, " 'On this rock I will build my church, and the powers of death shall not prevail against it' " (Matt. 16:18, RSV). In
the shadow of the cross Jesus declared, "Destroy this temple
[his body], and in three days I will raise it up" (John 2:19).

Quoting Psalm 118:22 he declared, " ' "The very stone which the builders rejected has become the head of the corner" ' " (Luke 20:17, RSV). He suggested that those who fall on this stone will be broken. It is quite apparent that Jesus also perceived of himself as a rock.

Is it any wonder then that Peter wrote:

> Come to him, to that living stone, rejected by men but in God's sight chosen and precious; and like living stones be yourselves built into a spiritual house, to be a holy priesthood, to offer spiritual sacrifices acceptable to God through Jesus Christ (1 Pet. 2:4-5, RSV).

Recall how Jesus in concluding the Sermon on the Mount admonished his hearers to be like the wise man and build on the rock (Matt. 7:24-27).

Surely these references demonstrate that the rock metaphor gathers up some of the central ideas of our faith. God is a rock. His Son is a rock. And we are becoming rocks.

I doubt that anyone would contend that God really is a rock. Even the pagans who worshiped before images of stone believed that the stone was a manifestation of a spiritual power. God is a rock in the metaphorical sense of having rock-like characteristics. It is of interest that although God is called a rock, he strictly prohibits any images being made of him.

"ROCK" SYMBOLIZES GOD

In preparing to write about the rock-likeness of God, I sought out a friend, Ed Leonard, who had spent many years as a rock cutter. Sure enough, he had given much thought to the metaphor. We concluded that rock symbolizes God in three ways: stability, strength, and salvation.

PERSONAL LEARNING ACTIVITY 26
Before studying further, write out how you feel the term *rock* can be used to symbolize the stability, strength, and salvation of God. Try to recall and write down at least one way the Scriptures use the term to symbolize each. Then continue your study to check your work.

Stability

We refer to stable friends as being "solid as a rock." We are more comfortable with people who can be counted on, who will not waver, who are steadfast.

"Solid as the Rock of Gibraltar," is another commonly used expression. This great mass of rock symbolizes stability in two ways: it has stayed in the same place and in the same shape for what seems to have been an almost endless period of time.

Builders of great buildings want to rest the foundation of their building upon solid rock. Explorers use rock formations as landmarks to guide them through the trackless wilderness. Families memorialize their dead with stone markers.

Sociologists and psychologists both suggest that modern man and the societies in which he lives are adrift on seas of uncertainty. Personally, and as nations, we crave order, stability, direction, and purpose. But our experience, individually and collectively, is one of chaos, conflict, disorder, and confusion.

Against this background the Scriptures declare: Our Lord is a rock. It seems evident that this is the message that the world needs. The God who is the same yesterday, today, and forever is the God who stands ready to meet our felt needs.

We like to sing:

> Great is thy faithfulness, O God my Father,
> There is no shadow of turning with thee;
> Thou changest not, thy compassions, they fail not;
> As Thou hast been thou forever wilt be.
>
> Great is thy faithfulness! Great is thy faithfulness!
> Morning by morning new mercies I see;
> All I have needed thy hand hath provided;
> Great is thy faithfulness, Lord, unto me![1]

And again:

> On Christ, the solid Rock, I stand; . . .
> All other ground is sinking sand.[2]

God's essential character is stable. He is great, good, and loving. We can count on him always to be himself. He is who he says he is; he wants of us what he says he wants; he does what he promises he will do.

The stable person is one whose character and actions match. God is not flighty; he does not play tricks on us. As was demonstrated in the early chapters, a central message of the biblical revelation is that our God is dependable. Read and meditate on Psalm 36 as a hymn to the dependability of God.

> Thy steadfast love, O Lord, extends to the heavens, thy faithfulness to the clouds. Thy righteousness is like the mountains of God, thy judgments are like the great deep; man and beast thou savest, O Lord. How precious is thy steadfast love, O God! The children of men take refuge in the shadow of thy wings. They feast on the abundance of thy house, and thou givest them drink from the river of thy delights. For with thee is the fountain of life; in thy light do we see light. O continue thy steadfast love to those who know thee, and thy salvation to the upright of heart! Let not the foot of arrogance come upon me, nor the hand of the wicked drive me away. There the evildoers lie prostrate; they are thrust down, unable to rise (Ps. 36:5-12, RSV).

Strength

Rocks are strong. Consider how diamonds have been used for the points of drills to cut through almost any substance, no matter how hard. Consider how the survival of early man was dependent on his skills in fashioning weapons from stones. With the hardness of rocks that he learned to propel, man was a match for animals that were larger and stronger than man. Consider how almost as soon as families began to settle in villages, they constructed stone walls for defense. These protected the village from marauders. Consider how uranium deposits, lodged in rocks, will provide the energy to fuel our civilization for years to come.

Through the centuries man has attached a special significance to mountains and the presence of God. I spent the summer of 1956 scrubbing pots and mopping floors at Glorieta Conference Center. What we sang to the campers was true: "In the midst of the mountains God's presence you'll find." And Glorieta Baldy stood towering above the campground as a symbolic reminder of the strength, power, and majesty of the creator God.

When I first visited the French Broad Baptist Church, these lines ran through my mind:

> I will lift up mine eyes unto the hills, from whence cometh
> my help. My help cometh from the Lord, which made heaven
> and earth. He will not suffer thy foot to be moved: he that
> keepeth thee will not slumber (Ps. 121:1-3).

Constructed of handmade brick and adorned with priceless
stained-glass windows, this country church is nestled on the
banks of Douglas Lake. As one arrives at the church, he looks
out across the lake at the majestic ruggedness of English Mountain and above and beyond it the peaks of the Great Smokies.
As my family and I worship there, I think of these lines; and
God is uniquely present with us.

The linking of mountains and Deity has a long history. When
the ancient Babylonians moved out of the mountains into the
plains of the valley of the Tigris and Euphrates Rivers, they
built artificial mountains to facilitate the worship of their traditional gods. So did the Aztecs as they moved into the valley of
Mexico. Zion, the mountain upon which Jerusalem and the
Temple were built, was the mountain where God was uniquely
present for the Hebrews.

Worshipers of God have learned that he is not localized in a
mountain or all mountains. Yet, we continue to find mountains
to be useful symbols for God's strength and his presence.

One of the most intriguing passages in the Scriptures is Hebrews 12:19-29. The writer asked the wavering believers
whether they would prefer to be the people of God as known at
Mount Sinai or at Mount Zion. He reminded them that God at
Sinai was foreboding, while at Zion (a reference to heaven)
God invited the redeemed to community with him. He was
asking whether they wanted to relate to God in terms of law
or in terms of grace. The wise choice is obvious. The relationship of grace with God who invites us to dwell eternally with
him is the only sensible choice.

Salvation
Jehovah, the God who is stable and strong, in himself, the God
we call mighty rock, offers us what humankind has sought in
and through rocks across the ages—salvation.

A refuge.—Rocks provide a place of refuge to which one can
flee in the face of a powerful enemy. No one would ever forget
a visit to the ancient capital of the Edomites and Nabataeans
—Petra. A natural fortress, it is surrounded on three sides by

steep mountain faces. On the fourth, steep cliffs drop off into the Great Rift Valley. The only practical entry is through a narrow gorge cut through a sandstone ridge by a seasonal stream. At points, the gorge, which is nearly a mile long, is only three to four feet wide. Petra was never captured by invaders because a handful of soldiers could withstand a mighty army in the narrow gorge. But the Nabataeans had taken the further protection of building a stronghold on top of a great rock that stood in the midst of the valley. Should their defense have ever been breached, they could have fled to the great rock.

The psalmist wrote:

> Lead thou me to the rock that is higher than I; for thou art my refuge, a strong tower against the enemy. Let me dwell in thy tent for ever! Oh to be safe under the shelter of thy wings! (Ps. 61:2-4, RSV).

God's presence in the warfare.—Rock tipped the weapons of the ancients as they fought against their adversaries, defensively or offensively. For centuries, the rock was mankind's basic weapon. Even today's metal weapons are simply improvements on the ancient forms.

The biblical concept of salvation is far richer than most of us realize. Influenced by modern individualism, we focus on personal salvation beyond this life. True, but God is also active in a saving way here and now. As was demonstrated by the rock analogy, God saves both as a place of refuge and as the leader of the forces of good in the conflict with the forces of evil. Consider some of the ways God is busy saving his people.

Christians affirm that God is active in history, moving toward his appointed ends. The satanic forces and our sin seem to affect the progress of God's plan. We interpret past events of history as the story of God's activities as he moves toward his goal. We know that because the incarnation made plain to believers what God had been doing in the history of Israel. We believe that Christ's return will make plain what God has been doing in the history of nations since then. Standing as we do in the midst of the unfolding story and knowing the end only by the barest of outline, we sometimes have difficulty interpreting what God is doing, especially when the side of evil seems victorious for a time. But based on what God did in bringing the old covenant to its completion, we trust that God is great enough and dependable enough to win the victory. Further, as his children we will share in his victory.

Not only is God working at the universal level of the processes of history, he is working uniquely with his church. Recall how rock imagery is used in the New Testament to speak of God's church. Christ, although rejected by the authorities, is the cornerstone. This does not mean a decorative piece into which various items are placed as in modern buildings. Rather it is the stone of beginning. Its placement determines the course, horizontally and vertically, of all the walls. Every stone is placed in relation to the cornerstone. Each believer is a stone to be placed in a great spiritual temple which honors God. Each is oriented toward the corner and is bonded to all the others. United they are something of great beauty and worth (1 Pet. 2:4-9).

This church is the New Israel. And like the old, God has saved it again and again from physical extinction. And as something spiritual God is saving it eternally. Congregations, movements, and orders may come and go, but the church marches on.

Application to believers' lives.—But where is God's salvation in the everyday life of believers?

PERSONAL LEARNING ACTIVITY 27
Life testifies to the fact that God's salvation does not exempt the believer from loss, suffering, and defeat. Before you study what the text says about how the salvation of God applies in the everyday life of the believer, write out your own explanation. Then study on to bring your understanding into sharper focus.

Problems arise when we narrow our perspective to the specific. Specific persons, groups, institutions, and relationships suffer, die, pass from memory. Of course, God saves believers by granting them life eternal.

Again, let us approach the question from the opposite side. Is God never there to save us when we feel a need for him? Of course he is. If he were not, belief in him would have vanished long ago. The problem is that God does not always operate on our time schedule, according to our values, by our plan, or in keeping with our interpretation of what is required.

Christians are not immune to troubles; but in face of troubles, they have a saving refuge, strong and secure.

God does save in his time, in his way, in terms of his purposes. This truth makes it possible for us to draw upon his strength and stability to face the problems of everyday life. In him we find meaning, rest, and hope.

In discussing the idea that God is a rock, one comes finally to see that the statement of Martin Luther has never been improved on:

> A mighty fortress is our God, A bulwark never failing;
> Our helper he, amid the flood Of mortal ills prevailing:
> For still our ancient foe Doth seek to work us woe; His craft
> and power are great,
> And, armed with cruel hate, On earth is not his equal.
> Did we in our own strength confide, Our striving would be
> losing;
> Were not the right Man on our side, The Man of God's own
> choosing:
> Dost ask who that may be? Christ Jesus, it is he; Lord Sabaoth, his name,
> From age to age the same, And he must win the battle.[3]

Perhaps our modern individualism makes us a little uneasy with what Luther is saying, but that is our problem; it does not diminish the truth of his insight. God is a rock, a fortress. Ultimately, he will win the victory at every level—cosmic, historical, individual. Although we may fall a casualty because Satan is strong, our occasional stumbling does not mean ultimate defeat. We have the promise of eternal life. And finally what else can we say? Faith in God is essentially faith that he can and will do what he says he will do. Knowing him as a rock of stability, strength, and salvation, we can trust in him.

CONCLUSION

In this chapter I have directed our attention to a metaphor that is used in the Bible to indicate something of God's character and work. God is a rock. Because of the importance of rock in the history of civilization, this is an honorable title.

The metaphor appears many times in the Scriptures. Significantly, when Christ acknowledged his messiahship at Caesarea Philippi, he referred to himself as "the rock upon which he will build his church." Christ is God incarnate.

Three meanings of this metaphor were suggested: stability,

strength, and salvation. The first two are important qualities of God's character. The third refers to God's work which is an outward manifestation of his character. In discussing God's saving work, I suggested that salvation involved God's activity at several levels. At the personal level, I stressed that the almost universal experience of believers is that God has been for them a rock of refuge and a defender in times of trouble. This is, of course, in addition to his act of saving us eternally.

God is "a Mighty Rock within a weary land." And those who meet him in the cross know the refreshment, restoration, security, and rest that comes from dwelling in his shadow, particularly at those times when the hot breath of the satanic forces can be felt on the backs of our necks.

I like this. I am sure that you do too. It is wonderful to know that our God is strong and stable against the satanic forces. But in the shadow of the cross and its refreshment comes the challenge to go forth with God as our shield to do battle with evil.

NOTES

1. "Great Is Thy Faithfulness." Words, Thomas O. Chisholm, 1923. Renewal 1951. Hope Publishing Co., owner. All rights reserved. Used by permission.
2. "The Solid Rock." Words, Edward Mote, 1832.
3. "A Mighty Fortress Is Our God." Words, Martin Luther, 1529; tr. Frederick H. Hedge, 1853.

Chapter 9

"Help Us Be More Like You"

The social sciences have informed us that persons learn by imitating others. We take on the mannerisms, actions, attitudes, values, goals, and various other characteristics of those we are around. In the language of sociology, these others are our role models. Typically we seek the approval of our models and other important persons. We hope they will compliment us on the way we do things. The term used by social scientists to designate these people is significant others. *The basic principle of Christian ethics is that God is to be our model or pattern and our significant other.*

Several of us were talking in the lobby of the men's dormitory at Hannibal-LaGrange College one Sunday evening in the spring of 1954. When I heard my name called out, I looked up to see my roommate limping in, obviously in great pain. With the help of several others, I got him to our room. Someone got a pan, salts, and hot water from our dorm parents so he could soak his swollen ankle. In spite of questioning, Larry, now the pastor of a prominent church in Missouri, would not reveal the cause of his injury. Only later did the story become known.

The previous week had been Christian Emphasis Week on the campus. The featured speaker, Nelson Reagan, was effective with college students. One of his most impressive techniques was what he called a pianologue. Seated at the piano in center stage of the college auditorium, he would talk while playing chords, runs, and parts of well-known tunes to emphasize and reinforce his comments. Occasionally he would rise and stroll around the stage, still talking. While strolling, he had the peculiar mannerism of putting his hands behind his head, as prisoners are sometimes pictured. He would close his eyes as if in deep thought, all the time still strolling.

Since Larry could play the piano passably well, he had decided he would present a pianologue for the edification of the good people at Mount Pisgah, one of his "halftime" churches. When he announced his plans for the evening service, a wave of excitement surged through the congregation. The telephone was used that afternoon. By time for evening worship, the auditorium was well filled.

Larry had spent the afternoon practicing in the church auditorium, so he was not unusually nervous as the service began. Sitting at the piano he launched into a dramatic presentation of Jesus' encounter with the Samaritan woman at the well. Using the piano effectively, he had the crowd hanging on his every word and gesture. Rising from the piano Larry began to stroll back and forth across the platform. Almost instinctively he put his hands behind his head, fingers intertwined; he closed his eyes. Unfortunately, the platform at Mount Pisgah was much smaller than the stage at the college. Just as Larry was reaching the conclusion of his message, he missed a step and fell off the platform, spraining his ankle as he fell.

The social sciences have informed us that persons learn by imitating others. We take on the mannerisms, actions, attitudes, values, goals, and various other characteristics of those we are around. In the language of sociology, these others are our role models. Typically we seek the approval of our models and other important persons. We hope they will compliment us on the way we do things. The term used by social scientists to designate these people as *significant others*.[1] For example, my five-year-old son Daniel idolizes Rocky, a teenager in our church. He tries to walk and talk like Rocky. He quotes Rocky as an authority on a variety of subjects. He beams whenever Rocky notices him. For Daniel, Rocky is a significant other role model.

The basic principle of Christian ethics is that God is to be our model or pattern and our significant other.[2] Most Christians realize this. An often used prayer-line is, "Help us to be more like you." In all likelihood, you have presented this petition to the heavenly Father. But have you ever considered systematically what it means to be like God?

MEANING OF BEING LIKE GOD

The scriptural basis for this concept of becoming like God is strong. In the midst of the law that was attached to the old covenant this statement appears:

> "You shall be holy; for I the Lord your God am Holy" (Lev. 19:2, RSV).

Characteristically, Jesus, while giving the ethical demands of the new covenant, repeated this goal for conduct in heightened form:

> "You, therefore must be perfect, as your heavenly Father is perfect" (Matt. 5:48, RSV).

Paul stressed the idea that God was his significant other, the one he strove to please:

> Just as we have been approved by God to be entrusted with the gospel, so we speak, not to please men, but to please God who tests our hearts (1 Thess. 2:4, RSV).

Elsewhere he declared Christ to be the head of every person and God to be the head of Christ. In this context he admonished the Corinthians in these words:

> Be imitators of me, as I am of Christ (1 Cor. 11:1, RSV).

Paul's point was that Christians should take on the characteristics, attitudes, and actions that one sees in Jesus.

A similar emphasis is found in Hebrews 12:1-14. The writer declared that we are to run life's race as Jesus ran it. This admonition should not be taken to mean that we are to be crucified at age thirty-three. Rather we are to assume the attitudes and values and cultivate the qualities that characterized Christ's person. What a role model! Consider our model!

CONSIDERING THE PATTERN

If God is characterized as being great, good, loving, and free, and if the Son is like him, then we should be able to find these characteristics in the Gospels. That is, as we consider the acts and the teachings of Jesus, these qualities should be evident. Let us examine some of the acts and the teachings of Jesus to see if they show that he, like the Father, is great, good, loving, and free.

Early Years

The early pages of the Gospels declare the greatness of the Christ child. Angelic announcements (Luke 1:26-38; Matt. 1:18-25; Luke 2:8-14), the great star (Matt. 2:1-12), and the witness of Simeon and Anna (Luke 2:22-38) tell his unique significance. The same is true of the visit to the Temple in Jerusalem when Jesus was twelve years of age (Luke 2:41-50).

Jesus began his ministry by being baptized (Matt. 3:13-17). There John attested to the greatness of Jesus as did the dove and the voice from heaven that said, "This is my beloved Son, in whom I am well pleased." The appeal of his person was apparent when Jesus chose his first disciples (John 1:35-51).

Beginning of His Ministry

The essential goodness of Jesus was demonstrated in his encounter with Satan on the mount of temptation (Luke 4:1-13). Further evidence was provided by his cleansing of the Temple (John 2:13-22; Mark 11:15-18). In the interview with Nicodemus (John 2:23 to 3:21), Jesus spoke of his position of power, as the Son. He continued by saying that the Son came so that humankind might know the truth and be freed from the consequences of God's righteous judgment. The incarnation makes manifest God's love.

Also during this early period occurred the first of several confrontations with the religious authorities over what they considered failure by him and his disciples to keep the law (Mark 2:18-22; John 5; Mark 2:23-28; 3:1-6; Luke 13:10-21; 14:1-24). Two important points are involved. First, Jesus respected the law of God (Matt. 5:17-20); but he realized that within the setting of everyday living, laws may come into conflict. When this occurs, the basic law must take precedence (Mark 2:27-28). Second, in the new era, the age of the kingdom of God that Jesus was proclaiming (Mark 1:14-15), humankind will have direct access to the truth of God's will in their hearts through the work of the Holy Spirit (Luke 11:13; 12:10-12; 16:14-18). In these confrontations Jesus declared his freedom and offered freedom to those who will follow him.

John was careful to stress in his Gospel that Jesus employed his power and exercised his freedom always with the awareness of being subordinate to God (John 5:19-46; 7:11-24,28-31; 8:21-59; 10:7-18). His power and freedom were not for his glory and personal benefit. Rather they were to glorify and benefit the Father.

Sermon on the Mount

In the Sermon on the Mount, Jesus spoke with the authority of a prophet, yet even greater. He brought together the concepts of freedom and subordination. We are to be obedient to our Father. He will care for us so that we will not need to be troubled about the things of everyday life (Matt. 6). The watchword is to "'seek first his kingdom and his righteousness'" (RSV); things will be added. He also said that true disciples will produce the good fruits of righteousness (Matt. 7:13-23).

In Matthew 11:16-19 Jesus said something significant about his freedom. He was not going to conform to the Jews' expectations of what a Messiah is to be like. By inference, God was his significant other. He would please God. In any case the Jews could not be pleased.

On several occasions Jesus internalized the concepts of goodness and badness. A heart right with God produces righteous acts (Luke 16:14-17).

One dominated by Satan, demons, or self may produce either evil or outwardly good acts (Matt. 12:22-27; Mark 7:15-23; Luke 11:37-54), but in either case the God who looks upon the heart judges our real motives. Jesus was good because his heart was submissive to the will of God (Mark 10:18; John 14).

Miracles

In a series of acts recorded in Matthew, Mark, and Luke, Jesus demonstrated his power over nature, the spirit world, and physical existence. He calmed the sea (Luke 8:22-25). He healed the Gerasene demoniac (Luke 8:26-39). He cured the daughter of Jairus (Luke 8:40-56). Interestingly, after these and related miracles, Jesus commissioned his disciples to go throughout Galilee exercising similar power (Matt. 9:35 to 11:1).

After feeding the multitude, Jesus referred to himself as the Bread and as the Water of life which meet the basic needs of humankind. The way to the Father is through the Son (John 6:44-51).

A second time the voice of God declared Jesus as his Son. At the transfiguration, God instructed the disciples to listen to his Son (Mark 9:2-8).

Parables and Other Teachings

Many of his parables stress the importance of obedience and subordination to God (Matt. 18:15-35; Luke 12:13-48; Matt. 20:1-16). So do Christ's pronouncements to the disciples (Luke 9:57-62; 17:6-10; Mark 10:13-16; Matt. 20:17-28; Luke 22:14-16; 14:34).

In his discourse on being the Good Shepherd, Jesus spoke of his love and the Father's love. The bond of love united them. This was the source of his power. He offered those who would be his disciples the protection of this love relationship (John 10:7-18). He taught that the whole of the old covenant is summed up in the commandments to love God and neighbor.

Apparently, as Jesus moved into the final phase of his ministry, he stressed more and more that he was the Messiah. He proclaimed the coming of God's kingdom and his role in its accomplishment (Luke 17:22-27; Matt. 22:41-46; 24:29-31; 25:31-32; 26:63-64; Luke 22:66-70).

The Last Week

Jesus began the final week before his crucifixion by coming to Jerusalem as King (Matt. 21:1-9). The crowds responded and sought to crown him. Although they wanted a war lord, Jesus saw himself as a Suffering Servant (John 12:20-50).

Among his many statements recorded from that week is a scathing denouncement of the religious leaders for their immorality (Matt. 23:13-39). He prophesied the coming of punishment on them and the city (Matt. 24—28).

He continued by stressing that the elect must be vigilant awaiting his return (Matt. 24:43-50). And he described a day when people will be rewarded for being righteous. The standard of judgment appears to be not so much orthodoxy as love manifested in meeting basic human need (Matt. 25:31-46).

At the Lord's Supper Jesus told his disciples that he had a new commandment for them: "That ye love one another; as I have loved you, that ye also love one another. By this shall all men know that ye are my disciples, if ye have love one to another" (John 13:34-35). The love of the Son, expressed in so many ways, became the pattern for the followers (compare John 14:1-24).

In the great climactic discourse recorded in John 14—17, the various qualities of God, as revealed in Jesus, are drawn together. Jesus spoke of his obedience to the Father. He declared that this life-style should characterize the life of the believers. He spoke of the love that bound him and the Father and the disciples together. He spoke of the power that he had used to glorify the Father. His disciples would receive similar power through the Holy Spirit so they would be able to continue his work. He spoke of truth that the Spirit would reveal to free them. And he prayed to God that they would be kept righteous and become sanctified through the truth of his word.

In the garden (Matt. 26:39) and on the cross (Luke 23:46), Jesus further demonstrated his commitment to God through his obedience to his will. As the resurrected Christ he is the firstfruits of the new covenant. He told the disciples that through the Spirit they would have power to further the cause of the kingdom (John 20:20-23). He again stressed the importance of love for one another (John 21). He commissioned and empowered them to share the gospel (Matt. 28:19-20; Acts 1:3-8). He promised to come again, this time with the consummation of the work of the new covenant (Acts 1:11).

This brief presentation of the evidence from the Gospels amply demonstrates that Jesus was a great, good, loving, and free person. Throughout his life, through his acts, his teachings, and his life-style, these qualities characterize his person. Further his followers are called to have these qualities. Certainly one of the functions of the incarnation must have been to demonstrate how to live this kind of life within the frame of space and time as we know it.

BECOMING LIKE GOD

In conversion a person is "born again" (John 3:1-21). He becomes a child of God (Rom. 8—9), an heir, a joint heir with

Jesus (Rom. 8; Gal. 4). He is given a new heart (Ezek.
11:19-20). He is to present his body as a spiritual sacrifice to
God (Rom. 12:1-2). His mind is to be on things above (Col.
3:1-4). He is to be obedient to his Father (1 Pet. 1:2,14-17). He
puts on the armor provided by God in order to do battle with
evil (Eph. 6:10-12). He produces spiritual fruits (Gal. 5:22-24).
His will and God's will are to be the same (Rom. 12:2). His life
becomes something that glorifies the Father (John 15:8-10).

Essentially two points are being made: (1) The believer is to
become like his Father. (2) He is to live a life of obedience to
his Father. Our model is the first and greatest of his sons,
Jesus. Like the Father and the Son we are to be great, good,
loving, and free.

Like Him in Greatness

We are born of God to greatness. Involved in an understanding of greatness is power and position. As children of God we
hold a position of greatness. Believers should delight in the fact
that they are children of the King. Yet Jesus taught that those
who are great in the kingdom will be those who serve (John
13). Our position is not one from which we are to "lord" it over
others; rather it is for service. Unlike the typical life-style of
nobility, the children of the King do not oppress others. Instead, we are to invite them to share in the inheritance (Luke
14:1-24).

God gives to his children gifts of power (1 Cor. 12—14). The
life of the first-century church was characterized by the manifestation of power through the believers for building fellowship. It is a great temptation to misuse our power by not
acknowledging its source or by not using it to God's glory.
However, believers should not hesitate to use that power. Jesus
empowered his disciples for service. The history of the church
is full of accounts of God's empowering other believers. We
should ask God to give us power. We should use the power he
gives for his glory.

The kingdom is coming. Jesus will come with power. We will
reign with him. We will share in his glory.

Like Him in Goodness

While preparing this manuscript I became increasingly aware

that the basic fact about God is that he is powerful enough to accomplish what he wills, and that he is dependable and will do what he says he will do. It seems that the basic trait of goodness is dependability. God has called us to be dependable persons (1 Cor. 15:58; Heb. 12:1-14).

One of the frustrations about church work is that some with whom we are working lack dependability. So often an excellent session or program is planned, but those who could benefit most are not present. I believe that one of our most difficult tasks is to help believers to be dependable.

A person who is basically dependable will display the other qualities of goodness. He will be righteous, just, and holy. At least this has been my experience with believers.

Like Him in Loving
God wills that his children be loving persons. Jesus commanded his disciples to love one another (John 15:12). Paul offered the classic definition of love (1 Cor. 13). He declared that love is patient, kind, long-suffering, joyful, and righteous. Maintaining a relationship with someone else is more important than defense of one's pride.

This kind of love cuts against the grain of the philosophy of life that characterizes the world. This is why it is so difficult to live the Christian life in this frame. Although the church teaches us to be loving and self-giving, the world teaches us to be self-seeking, prideful, and vain.

The church needs to be a fellowship of love. It must be the one institution in society characterized by true joy, happiness, peace, and contentment. In the fellowship of the church one must be able to find support, sustenance, kindness, compassion, and forgiveness. First John is devoted to an exposition of how love should be practiced in the church. Every church member should consider himself and his church in the light of this epistle.

Like Him in Freedom
Jesus offered his followers true freedom. The truth of the gospel liberates us (John 8:34-46). How? Paul the "apostle of freedom" elaborated on this. Humankind in its natural condition is in bondage to sin. The law does not help much; in fact, it seems

actually to compound the problem for some. People live in fear of death.

The gospel news is that God loves us. That he will forgive us of our sins, cleanse us, adopt us, and dwell with us is something exciting. We are liberated from the burden of guilt. With his help we learn to do his will and not to sin. His offer of eternal life gives us the courage to face death. We are truly free (Rom. 6—9). Therefore, we are in a position to provide moral leadership in this fallen world. There is nothing that the forces of evil can do to us that counts ultimately.

That God is great, good, loving, and free can be declared with certainty. In Jesus, God was living and teaching us to be great, good, loving, and free. The new birth is birth to greatness, goodness, love, and freedom.

CONSIDERING ADDITIONAL FACTORS

Too often our admonitions to be ethical stop with telling people to be good and loving. What we need is some specific guidance in applying the qualities of the Godlike personality to the real life situations of everyday life. I want to develop three specific suggestions.

Be Subordinate as Sons

Although we are called to be like God, we are not gods. There is a difference. Although we take on the qualities of God's person, we remain subordinate to him. He is the one who defines good and evil. He is the one who rules history. He is the one who will be dominant throughout time and eternity. God is the truly great, good, loving, and free one. We only approximate these qualities.

Specifically as subordinates we are to do his will. God calls us to tasks that fall within his plan. We are to follow his orders. Ask his Spirit to communicate with your spirit. Turn your will over to him. Offer your body as a sacrifice to him. Have the same mind as was in Christ.

Be Godlike in Roles

Within the various institutions of society—family, occupation, recreation, religion, and so forth—each one of us plays many roles. Each role we play is related to other roles; the related roles may be called a role-set. For example, a family is a set of roles—father, mother, children, and kin. Each role is played by a specific actor, who also has other roles to play in other sets. Each role comes with certain rights and duties.

What it means to be great, good, loving, and free must be specifically defined in terms of these role-sets. A father should use his power; he should be dependable, righteous, and just; he should love; and he should express his freedom appropriately in relation to his wife, children, and kin. The same is true for each member of the set.

An important task for Christians is to consider and to discuss what is appropriate conduct for each of the common social role-sets in our society. What does it mean to be great, good, loving, and free within the various roles prescribed by the political, industrial, business, educational, health care, religious, and professional realms?

Be Godlike in Growth

An important variable in how we express Godlike qualities is our growth toward spiritual maturity. As we grow we become aware of our spiritual nearsightedness. We all have blind spots. Our understanding of what it means to be a child of God is constantly changing.

We grow to be more like Christ through the experience of trying to be like Christ. We should be building constantly, learning how better to comprehend the situation, learning what being Christlike in a role means, and learning more about what his goals for our lives are.

CONCLUSION

Persons learn by imitating the actions of role models. We seek the praise of significant others. The message of the Christian ethic is that Jesus is our role model. God is the significant other whose praise we should seek.

A study of Jesus' life reveals that he was great, good, loving, and free; and he fulfilled the role of Savior within the frame of the life-situation that was his. Likewise we are to develop these characteristics in our roles and apply them to our life-situation. This is the pathway to spiritual maturity.

The specific application of this basic ethical truth needs to be worked out by those who perform these roles. God holds us responsible for our behavior. Be holy like your heavenly Father (Lev. 19:2; Matt. 5:48).

PERSONAL LEARNING ACTIVITY 28
This activity possibly will be the most significant one you complete in this study. On the facing page is a form you can use to make definite plans which, if carried out, can aid your personal growth. The four qualities of Godlikeness you have studied are listed on the form. Follow these steps to deal with each.

1. **Define the quality. State what you feel that quality is in terms of your life and your Christian experience.**
2. **Make an honest appraisal of the degree to which that quality is present in your life.**
3. **List several things you can do to foster the development and better use of the quality in your life.**

NOTES

   1. These are some of the basic concepts of the symbolic interactionist school of social psychology. See Ralph H. Turner, *Family Interaction* (New York: John Wiley & Sons, Inc., 1970).
   2. This point is made by H. Richard Niebuhr in *The Responsible Self* (New York: Harper & Row, Publishers, Inc., 1963), a classic in ethics.

A Plan for My Personal Growth

	For my own life, my definition of this quality is	How weaknesses and strengths of this quality in my life can be seen	What I will do to strengthen and better use this quality in my life
GREATNESS			
GOODNESS			
LOVING			
FREEDOM			

Conclusion

In introducing *The Doctrine of God*, I outlined the trip I proposed. We have come to the end of the journey. Looking back, what have we seen?

Baptists believe in the personhood of God. God, like all persons, has body, mind, conscience, and will. He is conscious of self. God is a Spirit person. As such he is both within and without the time/space frame of human experience. The godhead is comprised of three persons, different in function, yet complementary. They share a common essence. These three persons are known as Father, Son, and Spirit.

Like all persons, God is known through his acts, his pronouncements, and reflection by those who have been encountered by him. Four characteristics of his personality stand out: greatness, goodness, love, and freedom. As God, he has a position of great power. He demonstrates his power in his activities of creation, redemption, and perfection.

God has shown himself to be dependable, trustworthy, righteous, just, and holy. Consequently, we can declare that God is good. In his many mighty acts, but most particularly in the incarnation, God has revealed himself to be loving. Because God does not conform to our will but demands that we conform to his, we know that God is free.

Baptists also stress God's activity in four social roles—King, Judge, Father, Servant. A balanced view of God declares that he acts in all of these roles. As King, God creates, rules, and will win the final victory. As Judge, he rewards and punishes humankind justly. As Father, he seeks to redeem his fallen children. As Suffering Servant, he died that we might live.

This personal God encounters humankind. His Spirit and ours communicate. God wills that we be like him: great, good, loving, and free. His Spirit works with us toward those ends.

Rock is an apt metaphor for describing God's qualities. He is stable, strong, and saving.

God is active at several levels. Not only does he deal directly with persons, he also deals with groups, institutions, and nations. He is in control of history and is moving it toward his goals. Because God is working at so many levels, it is difficult to understand his actions. Yet, we are called to trust in him. Ultimately, he will make things right.

My hope and prayer is that this study will provide a kind of overview. Within it you can organize your regular study and worship of God. As you look more deeply into those facets of his person that particularly interest you, the whole of the structure of *The Doctrine of God* can serve as an anchor.

SMALL GROUP STUDY GUIDES
Bill Latham

SESSION 1

Introduction and Chapter 1

Session goal: By the end of this session members should have established an agreement about the way they will work together in this study. Also, each member should be able to explain the meaning of God's freedom in terms of his own life.

Preparation
● Prepare four sheets of newsprint as illustrated. Staple them to a cardboard back to form a flipchart.

● On a small table arrange a display that includes a Bible, *The Doctrine of God*, a copy of *The Baptist Faith and Message* by Herschel H. Hobbs, a hymnal, and at least one of the books referred to under Notes at the end of each chapter.

● Prepare three flash cards at least twelve inches long. Label them: *Baptists, Traditionalist, Radical.*

● Enlist three members to prepare and present a role-playing situation in which they engage in a heated discussion. One member who represents "Traditionalist" and another who represents "Radical" make the accusations discussed under "Baptists and the Freedom of God" in chapter 1. The person who represents "Baptists" answers with the Baptists' position (also discussed in the same part of chap. 1).

● Have pencils and paper available.

● Cut from colored poster board an arrow at least four inches long and glue a clothespin to its back.

Procedure
● Begin by recalling how the author compared planning a trip to the organization of the text and the way it should be studied.

DESTINATION

1. Who is God?

2. God is person.

3. Confessions/statements of faith

4. Everyday worship

5. Build the church

Page 1

MODE

1. Bible

2. The Doctrine of God

3. The Baptist Faith and Message

4. Hymnal

5. Other books

Page 2

ROUTE

God Is Free
God Is Great
God Is Good
"Praise Him . . . God Is Love"
"My God Is Real"
"In the Name of the Father . . ."
"We Want to Thank You, Lord, . . ."
"The Shadow of a Mighty Rock"
"Help Us Be More Like You"

Page 3

COST—BENEFIT

1. Preparation

2. Participation

3. Acceptance of others

4. Responsibility for others

5. Openness to growth

Page 4

● Show page 1 of the flipchart you have prepared. Use the material in "Destination" in Introduction and the Foreword to explain the author's general objectives.

● Show page 2 of the flipchart. Call attention to the display you have prepared and explain (1) that the nature of this study is exposition and (2) how these study aids will be used.

● Show page 3 of the flipchart. State the session goal for each session to give a brief preview of the study.

● Show page 4 of the flipchart and emphasize the following points:

1. It will be assumed that before each session, each person prepared by carefully studying the material in the text related to that session.

2. Success of the study depends largely on each member's participating in the learning activities planned for each session.

3. It is important that there be a freedom to express and a willingness to accept differing views.

4. This will be a joint learning experience. Members should feel responsible to help one another explore and learn.

5. Each person should approach the study with a willingness to learn.

● Ask members if they are willing to agree to this outline and these responsibilities as a working agreement to guide them in their approach to this study. If not, make whatever adjustments the group feels necessary to arrive at the group contract for this study.

● Return the flipchart to page 3 and place the arrow so that it points to the title for chapter 1. Ask members what concepts are involved in the idea that God is free. (See the first paragraph under "Baptists and the Freedom of God" in chap. 1.) Introduce the first person in the role playing. Give him the "Baptists" flash card, and state that he represents Baptists and their position on the freedom of God. Say: But Baptists have drawn criticism from both the traditionalists and the radicals. Introduce the other two members in the role playing and give them the appropriate flash cards to hold. Then have the three role-play their assignment.

● After the role playing, ask the group to discuss the meaning of God's freedom in terms of their own lives.

• Distribute pencils and paper, and ask each person to complete this statement: My God is free. For me, this means _____. After several minutes allow members who wish to do so to share what they have written.

SESSION 2

Chapter 2

Session goal: At the end of this session the group should have composed an answer to this question: How can a Christian know that his God is a great God?

Preparation
• Write the following work assignment on a chalkboard or on a piece of newsprint fastened to the wall with loops of masking tape: *Review chapter 2 and complete Personal Learning Activity 3.*
• Have the flipchart and arrow available.
• Label three sheets of newsprint: *Mighty Acts, Roles, Personality Traits.*
• Have additional newsprint available.
• Prepare three advance assignments slips:
Assignment 1: Your group is to prepare to lead a ten-minute Bible study to help members gain insights into how God's mighty acts show his goodness. (See chap. 2 of the text for help.)
Assignment 2: Same as Assignment 1 (except that "God's roles" should be substituted for "God's mighty acts").
Assignment 3: Same as Assignment 1 (except that "God's characteristics" should be substituted for "God's mighty acts").

Procedure
• As members arrive explain that a knowledge of chapter 2 is important to the work to be done during this session. Ask each person to begin work on the assignment you have written on the chalkboard or on newsprint. Allow this work to continue ten minutes into the regular session time.
• Ask, How would you explain the basis of your belief that God is a great God? Allow time for responses. Display page 3

of the flipchart with the arrow pointing to the title for chapter 2. State the session goal.

● Spend the entire period leading the group to formulate an answer to the question. Follow these steps:

First step: Have members suggest points and ideas that should be included in the answer. Ask a member to record all the suggestions.

Second step: Group the suggestions into categories. Suggest that since the text uses three categories, the group may want to use these also. Attach the three prepared sheets of newsprint to the wall. Ask if there are other categories that should be included. Write these on additional sheets and fasten them to the wall. Have the recorder read the suggestions made earlier. Have the group decide the category in which each suggestion belongs and write it on the appropriate newsprint.

Third step: Evaluate and adjust the suggestions. Perhaps group members will want to delete some and combine others.

Fourth step: Have the group use the suggestions on the adjusted lists to form an outline of their answer. Write this outline on the chalkboard or on another piece of newsprint fastened to the wall.

Fifth step: Have members compose their answer by making complete statements of the points and ideas in the outline. Have the recorder write each part of the answer as it is developed. You should be thoroughly familiar with the contents of chapter 2 so that you can direct the group to consider appropriate passages of Scripture as they work on different ideas in their answer.

● Divide the group into three work groups and make a record of the persons in each group. Give each group one of the advance assignment slips you have prepared. Have the work groups meet briefly to agree on a time before the next session to meet and prepare their assignments.

● Have the group sing "How Great Thou Art" to close the session.

SESSION 3

Chapter 3

Session goal: Through directed Bible study, members

should have gained insights into the meaning of God's goodness.

Preparation
- Have the flipchart and arrow available.
- Get extra Bibles.
- Get pencils and paper.

Procedure
- Give the work groups formed at the previous session ten minutes to complete their preparation. Have your list of work group assignments in case that information is needed. Any person not at the previous session should be assigned to a work group.
- Display the flipchart with the arrow pointing to the title for chapter 3. State the session goal and explain the procedure to be used in this session.
- Distribute pencils, paper, and Bibles to those who need them.
- Have each work group lead its assigned study. Keep up with the time, and do not allow a group to use more than ten minutes.
- After the three studies, use the remaining time for members to point out and discuss insights they gained as a result of the studies.

SESSION 4

Chapter 4

Session goal: By the end of this session members should have reviewed various expressions of God's love and stated what God's love in them should mean in terms of their relationships with other Christians.

Preparation
- Have the flipchart and arrow available.
- Enlist a member to introduce the study by giving in the form of a monologue the author's introduction.
- Enlist a member to explain and compare the meanings of *eros*, *phileo*, and *agape*.

• On a chalkboard or on a piece of newsprint fastened to the wall with loops of masking tape, write the chapter outline, except for "God's Love Makes Community Possible" and "Conclusion."

Procedure
• Call on the person enlisted in advance for the monologue introduction. Then display the flipchart with the arrow pointing to the title for chapter 4, and state the session goal.
• Display the chapter outline you prepared in advance. Lead the group in a brief review of the chapter by having them recall and briefly discuss each point in the outline and Scriptures related to it. Do not spend more than twenty-five minutes in this activity.
• Add to the chapter outline: God's Love Makes Community Possible. Lead the group to spend the remaining time discussing their answers to the questions in Personal Learning Activity 14.

SESSION 5

Chapter 5

Session goal: By the end of this session members should be able to explain in their own words what it means to encounter God as a person.

Preparation
• Display the flipchart.
• Prepare two pieces of newsprint. Label one *Essential Elements* and the other *Social Elements*.
• Prepare a chart as illustrated.
• Enlist a person to explain the relationships shown on the chart illustrated.

Procedure
• Begin by briefly recounting the chapter introduction in which the author tells of his courtship and marriage. Then show the flipchart with the arrow pointing to the title for chapter 5, and state the session goal.

GOD IS	GOD HAS
Great	Will
Good	Conscience
Love	Form

● Display the chart you prepared in advance. Call on the person enlisted to explain the relationships shown on the chart. After the report allow members to discuss the ideas presented.

● Point out that the text emphasizes that since God is person, we are to encounter him as a person. Ask, What should it mean in terms of Christian living and spiritual growth for believers to encounter their God person-to-person? Spend the remainder of the time discussing the answer to this question. Encourage members to share personal experiences they have had in encountering God as a person.

SESSION 6

Chapter 6

Session goal: By the end of this session each member should be able to answer this question in his own words: How do you harmonize the idea that God is one, yet three?

Preparation
● Display the flipchart with the arrow pointing to the title for chapter 6.

● Enlist a person in advance to lead a thirty-minute study of the Trinity as it is developed in chapter 6. This person should use chapter 6 in the text and chapter 3 in *The Baptist Faith and*

Message as resources. Plans for this study should include involving group members by having them locate and discuss Scriptures and underline key phrases in the quotations from "The Baptist Faith and Message" in the text. If possible, enlist your pastor to lead this study. If not, secure the most capable teacher available. Stress the fact that time for this study is limited to thirty minutes.

Procedure

● Recall the difficulty the author as a small boy had understanding the Trinity. Ask members to recall misunderstandings or difficulties they may have had.

● Call attention to the flipchart that you have displayed with the arrow pointing to the title for chapter 6 and state the session goal.

● Introduce the person enlisted to lead the thirty-minute study of the Trinity. After the study allow members to ask questions and discuss ideas that were developed during the study.

● Ask each member to write out his own answer to this question: How do you harmonize the fact that God is one, yet three? Allow time at the close of the session for members to share what they have written.

SESSION 7

Chapter 7

Session goal: By the end of this session members should be able to suggest replies to selected questions that seem to pose problems in relation to God's providence.

Preparation

● Display the flipchart with the arrow pointing to the title for chapter 7.

● Prepare four posters. Write on one: *If God is all-powerful, why does he permit sin in his world?* Write on the second: *If God is good, why does he permit suffering in his world?* Write on the third:

If God is the ultimate cause of all things, does this not mean he must predestine persons to hell as well as to heaven? Write on the fourth: *If what is to be will be, why shouldn't I just sit back and let it happen?* Display these on tables or on the walls in the room.

- Enlist three members to serve as a panel. See that they know the questions they are to discuss. Emphasize that they are not being asked to "give parts" or to prepare speeches but that *all* panel members are to enter into a discussion of *each* question.
- Arrange the room for the panel discussion.

Procedure

- Begin by reading from a hymnal the words of "God Moves in a Mysterious Way" or "Praise to the Lord, the Almighty."
- State that this session deals with God's providence and use the first paragraph under "Meaning of Providence" in chapter 7 to give the central idea in the meaning of God's providence. Call attention to the flipchart and state the session goal.
- Call attention to the posters you have displayed in the room. State that these questions related to God's providence are honest questions in the minds of some believers. Ask group members to listen to the following discussion carefully so they will be better able to deal with these questions later in the session.
- Introduce the panel members and sit with them at a table before the group. Moderate a discussion of the following questions:

1. What does the term *God's providence* refer to in addition to the fact that God provides for the needs of believers?
2. What is the difference in general and special providence?
3. What is the difference in ultimate and secondary causes?

- After the panel has discussed these questions, allow members to respond to and discuss what has been said.
- Call attention again to the four posters displayed in the room. Ask members to go to the poster that asks the question they are most interested in answering. Tell the groups they will have fifteen minutes to formulate a reply to their questions. Suggest that chapter 7 in the text is a good resource for their work.
- After fifteen minutes call for reports from the groups.

SESSION 8

Chapter 8

Session goal: By the end of this session members should be able to explain in their own words what the Scriptures are communicating when they say God is a rock.

Preparation
• Display the flipchart with the arrow pointing to the title for chapter 1.
  • Enlist a member to briefly explain why rocks, stones, and mountains were important to early man.
  • Get a chalkboard or sheets of newsprint.

Procedure
• Use the flipchart and arrow to lead a brief review of the study. Place the arrow so that it points to the title of chapter 1 and ask members to recall the most important ideas from that study. Follow the same procedure with each of the chapters through chapter 7.
  • Place the arrow so that it points to the title for chapter 8. Explain that this session deals with what the Scriptures are saying about God when they say he is a rock.
  • Call on a person enlisted to explain why rocks, stones, and mountains were important to early man.
  • Divide the chalkboard into three columns or fasten three sheets of newsprint to the wall. Ask members to recall the three qualities of God the Scriptures are describing when they call him a rock. (stability, strength, salvation) As these qualities are recalled, use them to label the columns on the chalkboard or sheets of newsprint. Lead members to discuss each quality —what it means in relation to God and what it means in relation to them as God's children. Be sure that in the discussion of salvation you lead members to deal with loss, suffering, and defeat in the life of a Christian.
  • If there is time, ask members to share briefly the benefits they feel they have received from this study.
  • Conclude the study by having the group sing "Beneath the Cross of Jesus."

SESSION 9

Chapter 9

Session goal: By the end of this session each person should have completed a plan which, if carried out, should foster his personal spiritual growth.

Preparation
• Display the unit chart with the arrow pointing to the title for chapter 9.
• Make copies of "A Plan for My Personal Growth" for members who may not have a text.

Procedure
• Begin by leading members to recall and enjoy again the story of Larry which begins chapter 9.
• Ask members to define *significant other* and name persons who have been significant others in their lives.
• Call attention to the flipchart and say: This session deals with the Christian's becoming more like God. State the session goal.
• Observe that, above all others, God should be the Christian's significant other. Briefly review the Scriptures under "Meaning of Being Like God" in chapter 9. Stress that these Scriptures say not only that the Christian is to become more like God but also that the best way to become more like God is to use Christ as the model.
• Ask members to take five minutes to review the section "Considering the Pattern" in chapter 9.
• Lead members to discuss these questions: In terms of our lives what does it mean to be like Christ in greatness? in goodness? in loving? in freedom?
• Ask members to work individually and complete Personal Learning Activity 28. Let this activity continue until ten minutes remain in the session. Allow members who wish to do so to share some of their work with the group.

THE CHURCH STUDY COURSE

The Church Study Course consists of a variety of short-term credit courses for adults and youth and noncredit foundational units for children and preschoolers. The materials are for use in addition to the study and training curriculums made available to the churches on an ongoing basis.

Study courses and foundational units are organized into a system that is promoted by the Sunday School Board, 127 Ninth Avenue, North, Nashville, Tennessee 37234; by the Woman's Missionary Union, 600 North Twentieth Street, Birmingham, Alabama 35203; by the Brotherhood Commission, 1548 Poplar Avenue, Memphis, Tennessee 38104; and by the respective departments of the state conventions affiliated with the Southern Baptist Convention.

Study course materials are flexible enough to be adapted to the needs of any Baptist church. The resources are published in several different formats—textbooks of various sizes, workbooks, and kits. Each item contains a brief explanation of the Church Study Course and information on requesting credit. Additional information and interpretation are available from the participating agencies.

Types of Study and Credit

Adults and youth can earn study course credit through individual or group study. Teachers of courses or of foundational units also are eligible to receive credit.

1. *Class experience*.—Group involvement with course material for the designated number of hours for the particular course. A person who is absent from one or more sessions must complete the Personal Learning Activities for each session missed.
2. *Individual study*.—This includes reading, viewing, or listening to course material and completing the specified requirements for the course.
3. *Lesson course study*.—Parallel use of designated study course material during the study of selected units in Church Program Organization periodical curriculum units. Guidance for this means of credit appears in the selected periodical.
4. *Institutional study*.—Parallel use of designated study course material during regular courses at educational institutions, including Seminary Extension Department courses. Guidance for this means of credit is provided by the teacher.

Credit is awarded for the successful completion of a course of study. This credit is granted by the Church Study Course Awards Office, 127 Ninth Avenue, North, Nashville, Tennessee 37234, for the participating agencies. Form 151 (available free) is recommended for use in requesting credit.

When credit is issued to a person on request, the Awards Office sends to the church two copies of a notice of credit earned. The original copy of the credit slip should be filed by the Study Course Records Librarian in the participant's record of training folder. The duplicate should be given to the person who earned the credit. Accumulated credits are applied toward leadership or member development diplomas, which are measures of learning, growth, development, and training.

Detailed information about the Church Study Course system of credits, diplomas, and record keeping is available from the participating agencies. Study course materials, supplementary teaching or learning aids, and forms for record keeping may be ordered from Baptist Book Stores.

The Church Study Course Curriculum
Credit is granted on those courses listed in the current copy of *Church Services and Materials Catalog* and *Baptist Book Store Catalog*. When selecting courses or foundational units, the current catalogs should be checked to determine what study course materials are valid.

How to Request Credit for This Course

This book is the text for a course in the subject area Baptist Doctrine.

This course is designed for 7½ hours of group study. Credit is awarded for satisfactory class experience with the study material for the minimum number of hours. If supervised practice or laboratory experience is appropriate and is used, two hours of such guided activity may be substituted for one hour of class time, provided that at least one half of the required hours is spent in classwork. A person who is absent for one or more sessions must complete the Personal Learning Activities for each session missed.

Credit is also allowed for use of this material in individual study and in lesson course study and institutional study, if so designated.

After the course is completed, the teacher, the Study Course Records Librarian, or any person designated by the church should complete Form 151 (Church Study Course Credit Request, Revised 1975) and send it to the Awards Office, 127 Ninth Avenue, North, Nashville, Tennessee 37234. Individuals also may request credit by writing the Awards Office or by using the special coupon on the last page of this book.

INSTRUCTIONS: If requested by the teacher, fill in this form and give it to him when the course is completed. If preferred, mail this request for course credit to

AWARDS OFFICE
THE SUNDAY SCHOOL BOARD, SBC
127 NINTH AVENUE, NORTH
NASHVILLE, TENNESSEE 37234

State Convention	Association

Indicate Type of Study (X)

☐ Class ☐ Individual ☐ Lesson Course ☐ Educational Institution

CHURCH

Church Name

Mailing Address

City, State, Zip Code

MAIL TO

Mail to (If Different from Church Address)

Street, Route, or P.O. Box

City, State, Zip Code

LAST NAME	FIRST NAME AND MIDDLE INITIAL	MRS. (X)	COURSE TITLE
			The Doctrine of God

Cut along this line